A

The
Mission of the Benedictine Order

Edited by HANNAFORD BENNETT

JOHN LONG'S CARLTON CLASSICS

PRICES:—Decorative Cover, 3d. net; Cloth, 6d. net;
Leather, 1s. net; postage, 1½d. per vol.

The first twelve only are bound in decorative paper covers

The Four Georges . . .	W. M. THACKERAY
Childe Harold's Pilgrimage .	LORD BYRON
Much Ado About Nothing .	SHAKESPEARE
Warren Hastings . .	LORD MACAULAY
The Life of Nelson . .	ROBERT SOUTHEY
Tales (Selected) . .	EDGAR ALLAN POE
Christabel, and other Poems .	S. T. COLERIDGE
A Sentimental Journey .	LAURENCE STERNE
The Blessed Damozel, and other Poems	DANTE G. ROSSETTI
On Heroes and Hero-Worship .	THOMAS CARLYLE
Sonnets and Poems . .	SHAKESPEARE
Rasselas . . .	SAMUEL JOHNSON
Sonnets and Poems . .	EDMUND SPENSER
Essays (Selected) . .	JOSEPH ADDISON
His Book . . .	ARTEMUS WARD
The Dunciad, and other Poems .	ALEXANDER POPE
English Humorists of the 18th Century	W. M. THACKERAY
The Jumping Frog, and other Sketches	MARK TWAIN
Songs . . .	ROBERT BURNS
Essays (Selected) . .	LEIGH HUNT
Letters of Junius . .	ANONYMOUS
Humorous Poems . .	THOMAS HOOD
Confessions of an English Opium Eater	THOMAS DE QUINCEY
A Voyage to Lilliput . .	DEAN SWIFT
Grace Abounding . .	JOHN BUNYAN
Critical Essays . .	MATTHEW ARNOLD
Poems . . .	PERCY B. SHELLEY
Mr Gilfil's Love Story . .	GEORGE ELIOT
Scenes from Harry Lorrequer .	CHARLES LEVER
Poems . . .	BEN JONSON
Essays or Counsels Civil and Moral	FRANCIS BACON
Minor Poems . .	JOHN MILTON
Selections . . .	EDMUND BURKE
Sonnets . . .	WM. WORDSWORTH
A Voyage to Lisbon . .	HENRY FIELDING
Essays . . .	JAMES A. FROUDE
Essays from the Edinburgh Review	FRANCIS, LORD JEFFREY
Discourses on Art . .	SIR J. REYNOLDS
Love Poems . .	ROBERT BROWNING
The Benedictine Order .	CARDINAL NEWMAN
Sesame and Lilies . .	JOHN RUSKIN
Miscellaneous Poems .	CHARLES KINGSLEY

Other Volumes in Preparation

JOHN LONG, Publisher, LONDON

The Mission of the Benedictine Order

By

John Henry, Cardinal Newman

With Biographical Introduction

by

Hannaford Bennett

London

John Long

Norris Street, Haymarket

MCMVIII

Biographical Introduction

A WRITER in a recent number of one of the reviews asked why it is that there are no great prose writers now; no writers to compare with Carlyle or Ruskin or Froude or Newman. With the question itself we are not concerned, but the inclusion of Newman among the great prose masters of his century is worthy of remark, inasmuch as purely theological writers are not usually among the stylists. But Newman was an exception; he was a great writer as well as a great preacher and a great scholar; and his history, his criticism, and his sermons will always be read for their style. The words that he employed to describe instrumental symphonies might be applied to describe his own writings; they seem to " have escaped from some higher sphere; they are the outpourings of eternal harmony in the medium of created sound; they are echoes from our Home; they are the voice of angels, or the Magnificat of saints, or the living laws of Divine Governance, or the Divine Attributes; something are they besides themselves, which we cannot compass, which we cannot utter." It was the mission of Newman in the words of Gladstone " to give to the religious thought of his time and country the most powerful impulse which for a long time it had received from any individual."

Newman's qualities may be traced from his descent. His father was of Dutch, but really of Semitic origin, whose name was once spelt Newmann; and his mother belonged to a French Huguenot family, called Fourdrinier, that had long been settled in London as engravers and paper manufacturers. Newman the elder was a partner in a banking firm and a small landed proprietor in Cambridgeshire; he was a man of much general culture, and had an hereditary taste for music of which he possessed a practical and scientific knowledge. John Henry Newman, the eldest of his six children, was born in London

on the 21st of February, 1801. Some years later
the bank failed, and the circumstances of the
family changed, but it was not before Newman
was well able to stand alone. From boyhood
Newman was of a religious and contemplative
disposition: "I used to wish the Arabian Tales
were true; my imagination ran on unknown
influences, on magical powers and talismans. I
thought life might be a dream, or I an angel, and
all the world a deception, my fellow-angels by a
playful device concealing themselves from me,
and deceiving me with the semblance of a
material world." When he was sixteen years of
age Newman obtained a Trinity Scholarship of
sixty pounds for nine years. Among his contemporaries at Oxford were Gladstone, Keble,
Pusey, Whateley and Hurrell Froude. He
hoped for honours with his B.A. degree, but being
called up a day sooner than he expected, he broke
down and had to retire; thus he passed only in
the lower division of the second class. But
Newman's personality from the beginning made
itself felt at Oxford. His tutor, Mr Short,

meeting his father one day, went up to him, exclaiming, "Oh, Mr Newman, what have you given us in your son!" When he was only twenty-one years of age he became Fellow of Oriel.

Newman considered his election as Fellow of Oriel as the turning point in his life. It raised him from obscurity, and placed him on an equality with the highest University society and intelligence. In a year or two he was ordained and appointed Curate of St Clement's Church, Oxford; and subsequently he became Tutor of Oriel and Vicar of St Mary the Virgin, Oxford. All the while his influence was steadily growing. His appointment to St Mary's was, he says, "like the feeling of spring weather after winter. I came out of my shell; I remained out of it until 1841." At St Mary's, Newman gathered round him the flower of Oxford. "We can hardly imagine the effect which they (his sermons) produced when they were delivered," writes Mr Herbert Paul. "The preacher's unrivalled command of English, his exquisitely musical voice, his utter unworldliness, the fer-

vent evangelical piety which his high Anglican
doctrines did not diminish, were not less moving
than his singular power, which he seemed to
have derived from Christ Himself, of reading the
human heart. The young men who listened to
him felt, each of them, as if he had confessed his
inmost thoughts to Newman, as if Newman
were speaking to him alone." In 1832 Newman
resigned the Tutorship of Oriel and started with
Hurrell Froude on a Mediterranean tour; during
the course of the journey he fell dangerously ill,
but "I shall not die; I have not sinned against
the light. God has work for me to do," he said.
It was upon his recovery at this period that he
composed the hymn, "Lead Kindly Light."

The year of Newman's return to Oxford from
his foreign tour was the year in which the
religious mind of England was plunged into the
controversies of the Oxford Movement; and in
a year or two it seemed as if the best intellect in
the Church was drifting towards Rome. Newman contributed the first of the *Tracts for the
Times*, and Tract succeeded Tract from New-

man, Pusey, Keble, Hurrell Froude and Isaac
Williams during the next eight years.   Principal
Shairp says of Newman at this time that " a
mysterious veneration had by degrees gathered
round him till now it was almost as if some
Ambrose or Augustine of older ages had re-
appeared.   In Oriel Lane light-hearted under-
graduates would drop their voices and whisper
' There's Newman.'   When with head thrust
forward and gaze fixed as though on some
vision seen only by himself, with swift noiseless
step he glided by, awe fell on them for a moment,
almost as if it had been some apparition that
had appeared."   *Tract Ninety* was the last of the
series.   It was condemned by the Board of Heads
of Houses, and Newman, who acknowledged the
authorship, retired to the seclusion of Littlemore.
At Littlemore he preached his last sermon as an
Anglican.   The end was not far off; he resigned
his Fellowship; and on October the 9th, 1845, the
day upon which Renan put off the clerical habit
of the Roman Catholic Church, Newman through
Father Dominic, an Italian Passionist friar, was

received into it. No similar event caused such consternation. Gladstone described his secession as a "much greater event than the secession of John Wesley," and believed that "it had never been estimated at anything like the full amount of its calamitous importance." And even so detached an observer as Disraeli stated many years after Newman had joined the Church of Rome, that it was "a blow under which the Church of England still reeled."

In a few months Newman left Oxford, and did not visit the University again for thirty-two years. He went to Rome and was ordained priest. Next he gathered round him his followers, and founded the Oratory of the Brotherhood of S. Philip Neri. The last forty years of his life were passed at the Oratory, Birmingham. The famous pamphlet war with Kingsley, and Newman's triumphant vindication of himself in the *Apologia pro Vitâ Suâ* was the main event of his life outside his activities on behalf of his Church. Henceforward he was regarded with reverence even by those who differed most from

him.   In 1877 his old college elected him an Hon.
Fellow, and next year he went to Oxford and
was received with great distinction.   The Pope
made him a Cardinal.   In his last days Newman
returned more and more to his mother's simplicity of faith and life; his rooms at the Oratory
were more like the cell of a monk than the rooms
of a Prince of the Church.   Newman died on
August the 9th, 1890, and was buried at Rednal,
in the same grave as Father Ambrose St John,
" my life under God," he said, " for thirty-two
years."

HANNAFORD BENNETT

The Mission of the Benedictine Order

As the physical universe is sustained and carried on in dependence on certain centres of power and laws of operation, so the course of the social and political world, and of that great religious organisation called the Catholic Church, is found to proceed for the most part from the presence or action of definite persons, places, events, and institutions, as the visible cause of the whole.   There has been but one Judæa, one Greece, one Rome; one Homer, one Cicero; one Cæsar, one Constantine, one Charlemagne.   And so, as regards Revelation, there has been one St John the Divine, one Doctor of the Nations.   Dogma runs along the line of Athanasius, Augustine, Thomas.   The conversion of the heathen is ascribed, after the Apostles, to champions of the truth so few, that we may almost count them, as Martin, Patrick, Augustine, Boniface.   Then there is St Antony, the father of Monachism; St Jerome, the interpreter of Scripture; St Chrysostom, the great preacher.

15

Education follows the same law: it has its history in the Church, and its doctors or patriarchs in that history. This is the subject on which we propose to make some remarks in the pages which follow, taking Education in its broadest and most general sense, as the work contemplated in the august command, " Go, teach all nations," and as more or less connected with civilisation, social advance, the cultivation of learning, sacred and profane, and similar great facts, which are its historical interpretation.

The outline of what we have to say on the subject is simple enough; it is the filling up of details which will demand diligence in the writer, and patience in the reader. There are three main periods, then, of ecclesiastical history,—the ancient, the mediæval, and the modern; so far is plain: and there are three Religious Orders in those periods respectively, which succeed, one the other, on the public stage, and represent the teaching of the Catholic Church during the time of their ascendency. The first period is that long series of centuries during which society was breaking, or had broken up, and then slowly attempted its own reconstruction; the second may be called the period of reconstruction; and the third dates from the Reformation, when that peculiar movement of mind commenced, the issue of which is still to come. Now, St Benedict is the Patriarch of the ancient world; St Dominic of the mediæval; and St Ignatius of the modern. And in saying this, we are in no degree disrespectful to the Augustinians, Carmelites, Franciscans, and other great religious families which might be named; for we are not reviewing the whole history of Christianity, but selecting a particular aspect of it.

Perhaps as much as this will be granted to us without great hesitation. Next we proceed, after thus roughly mapping out our view of history, roughly to colour it, by way of contrasting these three patriarchs of Christian teaching with each other. To St Benedict then, who may fairly be taken to represent the various families of monks before his time and those which sprang from him (for they are all pretty much of one school), to this great saint let us assign, for his discriminating badge, the Poetical; to St Dominic, the Scientific; and to St Ignatius, the Practical and Useful.

These characteristics, which belong respectively to the works of the three great Masters, grow out of the circumstances under which they respectively entered upon them. Benedict, entrusted with his mission almost as a boy, infused into it the romance and simplicity of boyhood. Dominic, a man of forty-five, a graduate in theology, a priest and a canon, brought with him into religion the maturity and completeness of learning, which he had acquired in the schools. Ignatius, a man of the world before his conversion, transmitted as a legacy to his disciples that knowledge of mankind which cannot be learned in cloisters. And thus

B

the three several Orders were (so to say) begotten
in Poetry, Science, and Good Sense.

And here another coincidence suggests itself.
We have been giving these three attributes to the
three Patriarchs severally, from a *bona fide* regard
to their history, and without at all having any theory
of philosophy in our eye. But, after having so
described them, it certainly did strike us that we
had unintentionally been illustrating a somewhat
popular notion of the day, the like of which is
attributed to authors with whom we have as little
sympathy as with any persons who can be named.
According to these speculators, the life, whether of
a race or of an individual of the great human family,
is divided into three stages, each of which has its
own ruling principle and characteristic. The
youth makes his start in life, with " *hope* at the
prow, and *fancy* at the helm; " he has nothing else
but these to impel or direct him; he has not lived
long enough to exercise his reason, or to gather in
a store of facts; and, because he cannot do otherwise, he dwells in a world which he has created.
He begins with illusions. Now, facts are external
to him, but his reason is his own: of the two, then,
it is easier for him to exercise his reason than to
ascertain facts. Accordingly, his first mental
revolution, when he discards the life of aspiration
and affection, which has disappointed him, and the
dreams of which he has been the sport and victim,
is to embrace a life of logic: this then is his second
stage,—the metaphysical. He acts now on a plan,

thinks by system, is cautious about his middle terms, and trusts nothing but what takes a scientific form. His third stage is when he has made full trial of life; when he has found his theories break down under the weight of facts, and experience falsify his most promising calculations. Then the old man recognises at length, that what he can taste, touch, and handle, is trustworthy, and nothing beyond it. Thus he runs through his three periods of Imagination, Reason, and Sense; and then he comes to an end, and is not;—a most impotent and melancholy conclusion.

We repeat, we have no sympathy in so heartless a view of life, and yet it seems to square with what we have been saying of the three great Patriarchs of Christian teaching. And certainly there is a truth in it, which gives it its plausibility. However, we are not concerned here to do more than to put our finger on the point at which we diverge from it, in what we have been saying and must say concerning them. It is true, then, that history, as viewed in these three saints, is, somewhat after the manner of the theory we have mentioned, a progress from poetry through science to practical sense or prudence; but then this important *proviso* has to be borne in mind at the same time, that what the Catholic Church once has had, she never has lost. She has never wept over, or been angry with, time gone and over. Instead of passing from one stage of life to another, she has carried her youth and middle age along with her, on to her latest time. She has not changed possessions, but accumulated them, and has brought out of her treasure-house, according to the occasion, things new and old. She did not lose Benedict by finding Dominic; and she has still both Benedict and Dominic at home, though she has become the mother of Ignatius. Imagination, Science, Prudence, all are good, and she has them all. Things incompatible in nature, coexist in her; her prose is poetical on the one hand, and philosophical on the other.

Coming now to the historical proof of the contrast we have been instituting, we are sanguine in thinking that one branch of it is already allowed by the consent of the world, and is undeniable. By common consent, the palm of Prudence, in the full sense of that comprehensive word, belongs to the School of Religion, of which St Ignatius is the Founder. That great Society is the classical seat and fountain of discretion, practical sense, and wise government. Sublimer conceptions or more profound speculations may have been elaborated elsewhere; but, whether we consider the illustrious Body in its own constitution, or in its rules for instruction and direction, we see that it is its very genius to prefer this most excellent prudence to every other gift, and to think little both of poetry and of science, unless they happen to be useful. It is true that, in the long catalogue of its members, there are to be found the names of the most consummate theologians, and of scholars the most elegant and accomplished; but we are speaking here, not of individuals, but of the body itself. It is plain, that the body is not over-jealous about its theological conditions; or it certainly would not suffer Suarez to controvert with Molina, Viva with Vasquez, Passaglia with Petavius, and Faure with Suarez, De Lugo, and Valentia. In this intellectual freedom its members justly glory; inasmuch as they have set their affections, not on the opinions of the Schools, but on the souls of men. And it is the same charitable motive which makes them give up the poetry of life, the poetry of ceremonies, —of the cowl, the cloister, and the choir,—content with the most prosaic architecture, if it be but convenient, and the most prosaic neighbourhood, if it be but populous. We need not then dwell longer on this wonderful Religion, but may confine the remarks which are to follow, to the two Religions which historically preceded it — the Benedictine and the Dominican.

One preliminary more, suggested by a purely fanciful analogy:— As there are three great Patriarchs on the high road and public thoroughfare of Christian History, so there were three chief Patriarchs in the first age of the chosen people. Putting aside Noe and Melchisedec, and Joseph and his brethren, we recognise three venerable fathers,—Abraham, Isaac, and Jacob: Abraham, the father of many nations; Isaac the intellectual, living in solitary simplicity, and in loving contemplation; and Jacob, the persecuted and helpless, visited by marvellous providences, driven from place to place, set down and taken up again, ill-treated by those who were his debtors, and maligned when he is innocent, yet carried on and triumphing amid all troubles by means of his most faithful and powerful guardian-archangel. We are exempted, by what has gone before, from the duty of completing our parallel, in the instance of Jacob; but, as to Benedictines and Dominicans, we shall introduce them successively under the type, as it may be called, of Abraham and Isaac.

St Benedict, like the great Hebrew Patriarch, was the "Father of many nations." He has been styled "the Patriarch of the West," a title which there are many reasons for ascribing to him. Not only was he the first to establish a perpetual Order of Regulars in Western Christendom; not only, as coming first, has he had an ampler course of centuries for the multiplication of his children; but his Rule, as that of St Basil in the East, is the normal rule of the first ages of the Church, and was in time generally received even in communities which in no sense owed their origin to him. Moreover, out of his Order rose, in process of time, various new monastic families, which have established themselves as independent institutions, and are able to boast in their turn of the number of their houses, and the sanctity and historical celebrity of their members. He is the representative of Latin monachism for the long extent of six centuries, while monachism was one; and even

when at length varieties arose, and distinct titles
were given to them, the change grew out of him;—
not the act of strangers who were his rivals, but of
his own children, who did but make a new beginning in all devotion and loyalty to him. He died
in the early half of the sixth century; at the
beginning of the tenth rose from among his French
monasteries the famous Congregation of Cluni,
illustrated by St Majolus, St Odilo, Peter the
Venerable, and other considerable personages,
among whom is Hildebrand, afterwards Pope
Gregory the Seventh. Then came, in long succession, the Orders or Congregations of Camaldoli
under St Romuald, of Vallombrosa, of Citeaux, to
which St Bernard has given his name, of Monte
Vergine, of Fontvrault; those of England, Spain,
and Flanders; the Silvestrines, the Celestines, the
Olivetans, the Humiliati, besides a multitude of
institutes for women, as the Gilbertines and the
Oblates of St Frances, and then at length, to
mention no others, the Congregation of St Maur
in modern times, so well known for its biblical,
patristical, and historical works, and for its learned
members, Montfaucon, Mabillon, and their companions. The panegyrists of this illustrious Order
are accustomed to claim for it in all its branches as
many as thirty-seven thousand houses, and,
besides numerous Popes, 200 Cardinals, 4 Emperors,
46 Kings, 51 Queens, 1406 Princes, 1600 Archbishops, 600 Bishops, 2400 Nobles, and 15,000
Abbots and learned men.

Nor are the religious bodies which sprang from
St Benedict the full measure of what he has accomplished,—as has been already observed. His Rule
gradually made its way into those various monasteries, which were of an earlier or an independent
foundation. It first coalesced with, and then
supplanted, the Irish Rule of St Columban in
France, and the still older institutes which had been
brought from the East by St Athanasius, St
Eusebius, and St Martin. At the beginning of the
ninth century it was formally adopted throughout
the dominions of Charlemagne. Pure, or with
some admixture, it was brought by St Augustine
to England; and that admixture, if it existed,
was gradually eliminated by St Wilfrid, St Dunstan,
and Lanfranc, till at length it was received, with
the name and obedience of St Benedict, in all the
Cathedral monasteries (to make no mention of
others), excepting Carlisle. Nor did it cost such
regular bodies any very great effort to make the
change, even when historically most separate from
St Benedict; for the Saint had taken up for the
most part what he found, and his Rule was but
the expression of the genius of monachism in those
first ages of the Church, with a more exact adaptation to their needs than could elsewhere be found.

So uniform indeed had been the monastic idea
before his time, and so little stress had been laid
by individual communities on their respective
peculiarities, that religious men passed at pleasure
from one body to another. St Benedict provides

in his Rule for the case of strangers coming to one of his houses, and wishing to remain there. If such a one came from any monastery with which the monks had existing relations, then he was not to be received without letters from his Abbot; but, in the instance of "a foreign monk from distant parts," who wished to dwell with them as a guest, and was content with their ways, and conformed himself to them, and was not troublesome, "should he in the event wish to stay for good," says St Benedict, "let him not be refused; for there has been room to make trial of him, during the time that hospitality has been shown him: nay, let him even be invited to stay, that others may gain a lesson from his example; for in every place we are servants of one Lord and soldiers of one King."

The unity which these words imply as the distinctive token of a monk in every part of Christendom, may be described as a unity of object, of state, and of occupation. Monachism was one and the same everywhere, because it was a reaction from that secular life which has everywhere the same structure and the same characteristics. And, since that secular life contained in it many objects, many states, and many occupations, here was a special reason, as a matter of principle, why the reaction from it should bear the badge of unity, and should be in outward appearance one and the same everywhere. Moreover, since that same secular life was, when monachism arose, more than ordinarily marked by variety, perturbation, and confusion, it seemed on that very account to justify emphatically a rising and revolt against itself, and a recurrence to some state, which, unlike itself, was constant and unalterable. It was indeed an old, decayed, and moribund world, into which Christianity had been cast. The social fabric was overgrown with the corruptions of a thousand years, and was held together, not so much by any common principle, as by the strength of possession and the tenacity of custom. It was too large for public spirit, and too artificial for patriotism, and its many religions did but foster in the popular mind division and scepticism. Want of mutual confidence would lead to despondency, inactivity, and selfishness. Society was in the slow fever of consumption, which made it restless in proportion as it was feeble. It was powerful, however, to seduce and deprave; nor was there any *locus standi* from which to combat its evils; and the only way of getting on with it was to abandon principle and duty, to take things as they came, and to do as the world did. Worse than all, this encompassing, entangling system of things was, at the time we speak of, the seat and instrument of a paganism, and then of heresies, not simply contrary, but bitterly hostile, to the Christian name. Serious men not only had a call, but every inducement which love of life and freedom could inspire, to escape from its presence and its sway.

Their one idea then, their one purpose, was to be

quit of it; too long had it enthralled them. It was not a question of this or that vocation, of the better deed, of the higher state, but of life and death. In other times a variety of holy objects might present themselves for devotion to choose from, such as the care of the poor, or of the sick, or of the young, the redemption of captives, or the conversion of the barbarians; but early monachism was flight from the world, and nothing else. The troubled, jaded, weary heart, the stricken, laden conscience, sought a life free from corruption in its daily work, free from distraction in its daily worship; and it sought employments, as contrary as possible to the world's employments, —employments, the end of which would be in themselves, in which each day, each hour, would have its own completeness;—no elaborate undertakings, no difficult aims, no anxious ventures, no uncertainties to make the heart beat, or the temples throb, no painful combination of efforts, no extended plan of operations, no multiplicity of details, no deep calculations, no sustained machinations, no suspense, no vicissitudes, no moments of crisis or catastrophe;—nor again any subtle investigations, nor perplexities of proof, nor conflicts of rival intellects, to agitate, harass, depress, stimulate, weary, or intoxicate the soul.

Hitherto we have been using negatives to describe what the primitive monk was seeking; in truth monachism was, as regards the secular life and all that it implies, emphatically a negation, or, to use

another word, a *mortification* ; a mortification of
sense, and a mortification of reason.   Here a word
of explanation is necessary.   The monks were too
good Catholics to deny that reason was a divine
gift, and had too much common sense to think to
do without it.   What they denied themselves was
the various and manifold exercises of the reason;
and on this account, because such exercises were
excitements.   When the reason is cultivated, it
at once begins to combine, to centralise, to look
forward, to look back, to view things as a whole,
whether for speculation or for action; it practises
synthesis and analysis, it discovers, it invents.   To
these exercises of the intellect is opposed simplicity,
which is the state of mind which does not combine,
does not deal with premises and conclusions, does
not recognise means and their end, but lets each
work, each place, each occurrence stand by itself,—
which acts towards each as it comes before it,
without a thought of anything else.   This simplicity is the temper of children, and it is the
temper of monks.   This was their mortification of
the intellect; every man who lives must live by
reason, as every one must live by sense; but, as it
is possible to be content with the bare necessities
of animal life, so is it possible to confine ourselves
to the bare ordinary use of reason, without caring
to improve it or make the most of it.   These monks
held both sense and reason to be the gifts of
heaven, but they used each of them as little as
they could help, reserving their full time and their

whole selves for devotion;—for, if reason is better than sense, so devotion they thought to be better than either; and, as even a heathen might deny himself the innocent indulgences of sense in order to give his time to the cultivation of the reason, so did the monks give up reason, as well as sense, that they might consecrate themselves to divine meditation.

Now, then, we are able to understand how it was that the monks had a unity, and in what it consisted. It was a unity, we have said, of object, of taste, and of occupation. Their object was rest and peace; their state was retirement; their occupation was some work that was simple, as opposed to intellectual, viz., prayer, fasting, meditation, study, transcription, manual labour, and other unexciting, soothing employments. Such was their institution all over the world; they had eschewed the busy mart, the craft of gain, the money-changer's bench, and the merchant's cargo. They had turned their backs upon the wrangling forum, the political assembly, and the pantechnicon of trades. They had had their last dealings with architect and habit-maker, with butcher and cook; all they wanted, all they desired, was the sweet soothing presence of earth, sky, and sea, the hospitable cave, the bright running stream, the easy gifts which mother earth, " justissima tellus," yields on every little persuasion. " The monastic institute," says the biographer of St Maurus, " *demands the most perfect quietness ;* " and where was quietness to be found, if not in reverting to the original condition of man, as far as the changed circumstances of our race admitted, in having no wants of which the supply was not close at hand; in the "nil admirari;" in having neither hope nor fear of anything below; in daily prayer, daily bread, and daily work, one day being just like another, except that it was one step nearer than the day before it to that great Day, which would swallow up all days, the day of ever-lasting rest?

However, we have come into collision with a great authority, M. Guizot, and we must stop the course of our argument to make our ground good against him. M. Guizot, then, makes a distinction between monachism in its birthplace, in Egypt and Syria, and that Western institute, of which we have made St Benedict the representative. He allows that the Orientals mortified the intellect, but he considers that Latin monachism was the seat of considerable mental activity. "The desire for retirement," he says, "for contemplation, for a marked rupture with civilised society, was the source and fundamental trait of the Eastern monks: in the West, *on the contrary*, and especially in Southern Gaul, where, at the commencement of the fifth century, the principal monasteries were founded, it was in order to live in common, *with a view to conversation* as well as to religious edifica-tion, that the first monks met. The monasteries of Lerins, of St Victor, and many others, were especially great schools of theology, the focus of

intellectual movement. It was by no means with
solitude or with mortification, but with discussion
and activity, that they there concerned themselves."
Great deference is due to an author so learned, so
philosophical, so honestly desirous to set out
Christianity to the best advantage; yet, we are at
a loss to understand what has led him to make
such a distinction between the East and West, and
to assign to the Western monks an activity of
intellect, and to the Eastern a love of retirement.

It is quite true that instances are sometimes to
be found of monasteries in the West, distinguished
by much intellectual activity, but more, and more
striking, instances are to be found of a like phenomenon in the East. If, then, such particular
instances are to be taken as fair specimens of the
state of Western monachism, they are equally fair
specimens of the state of Eastern also; and the
Eastern monks will be proved more intellectual
than the Western, by virtue of that greater interest
in doctrine and in controversy which given individuals or communities among them have exhibited.
A very cursory reference to ecclesiastical history
will be sufficient to show us that the fact is as we
have stated it. The theological sensitiveness of
the monks of Marseilles, Lerins, or Adrumetum,
it seems, is to be a proof of the intellectualism
generally of the West: then, why is not the greater
sensitiveness of the Scythian monks at Constantinople, and of their opponents the Acœmetæ, an
evidence in favour of the East? These two bodies

of Religious Orders actually came all the way from
Constantinople to Rome to denounce one another,
besieging, as it were, the Holy See, and the former
of them actually attempting to raise the Roman
populace against the Pope, in behalf of its own
theological tenet.   Does not this show activity of
mind? We venture to say, that, for one intellectual
monk in the West, a dozen might be produced in
the East.   The very reproach, so freely thrown out
by secular historians against the Greeks, of over-
subtlety of intellect, applies, if to any men, to
certain classes or certain communities of Eastern
monks. Sometimes they were enthusiastically
orthodox, quite as often furiously heretical.   If
Pelagius be a monk in the West, on the other hand,
Nestorius and Eutyches, both heresiarchs, are both
monks in the East; and Eutyches, at the time of
his heresy, was an old monk into the bargain, who
had been thirty years abbot of a convent, and
whom age, if not sanctity, might have saved from
this abnormal use of his reason.   His partisans
were principally monks of Egypt; and they, coming
up in force to the pseudo-synod of Ephesus, kicked
to death the Patriarch of Constantinople, and put
to flight the Legate of the Pope, and all this out of
a keen susceptibility about an intellectual opinion.
A century earlier, Arius, on starting, carried away
into his heresy as many as seven hundred nuns;
what have the Western convents to show, in the
way of controversial activity, comparable with a
fact like this?   We do not insist on the zealous

and influential orthodoxy of the monks of Egypt, Syria, and Asia Minor in the fourth century, because it was probably nothing else but an honourable adhesion to the faith of the Church; but turn to the great writers of Eastern Christendom, and consider how many of them at first sight are monks:— Chrysostom, Basil, Gregory, Nazianzen, Epiphanius, Ephrem, Amphilochius, Isidore of Pelusium, Theodore, Theodoret, perhaps Athanasius. Among the Latin writers no names occur to us but those of Jerome and Pope Gregory; we may add Paulinus, Sulpicius, and Cassian, but Jerome is the only learned writer among them. We have a difficulty, then, in comprehending, not to speak of admitting, M. Guizot's assertion, a writer who does not commonly speak without a meaning or a reason.

But, after all, however the balance of intellectualism may lie between certain convents or individuals in the East and the West, such particular instances are nothing to the purpose, when taken to measure the state of the great body of the monks; certainly not in the West, with which in this paper we are exclusively concerned. In taking an estimate of the Benedictines, we need not trouble ourselves about the state of monachism in Egypt, Syria, Asia Minor, and Constantinople, at least after the fourth century, by the end of which time the tradition had passed from the East to the West. Now, the Eastern monks of the fourth century simply follow the defined and promulgated doctrine of the Church; their intellectualism proper begins

c

with the fifth. Taking, then, the great tradition
of St Antony, St Pachomius, and St Basil in the
East, and tracing it into the West by the hands
of St Athanasius, St Martin, and their contemporaries, we shall find no historical facts but what admit
of a fair explanation, consistent with the views
which we have laid down above about monastic
simplicity, bearing in mind always, what holds
in all matters of fact, that there never was a rule
without its exceptions.

Every rule has its exceptions; but, further than
this, when exceptions occur, they are likely to be
great ones. This is no paradox; illustrations of it
are to be found everywhere. For instance, we
may conceive a climate very fatal to children, and
yet those who escape growing up to be strong men;
and for a plain reason, because those alone could
have passed the ordeal who had robust constitu-
tions. Thus the Romans, so jealous of their
freedom, when they resolved on the appointment
of a supreme ruler for an occasion, did not do the
thing by halves, but made him a Dictator. In like
manner, a trifling occurrence, or an ordinary
inward impulse, will be powerless to snap the bond
which keeps the monk fast to his cell, his oratory,
and his garden. Exceptions, indeed, may be few,
because they *are* exceptions, but they will be great.
It must be a serious emergence, a particular
inspiration, a sovereign command, which brings
the monk into political life; and he will be sure
to make a great figure in it, else why should he

have been torn from his cloister at all? This will
account for the career of St Gregory the Seventh or
of St Dunstan, of St Bernard or of Abbot Suger,
as far as it was political: the work they had to do
was such as none could have done but a monk with
his superhuman single-mindedness and his pertin-
acity of purpose. Again, in the case of St Boniface,
the Apostle of Germany, and in that of others of
the missionaries of his age, it seems to have been
a particular inspiration which carried them abroad;
and it is observable after all how soon most of them
settled down into the mixed character of agriculturalists and pastors in their new country, and
resumed the tranquil life to which they had originally devoted themselves. As to the early Greek
Fathers, some of those whom we have instanced
above are only *prima facie* exceptions, as
Chrysostom, who, though he lived with the monks
most austerely for as many as six years, can hardly
be said to have taken on himself the responsibilities
of their condition, or to have simply abandoned
the world. Others of them, as Basil, were scholars,
philosophers, men of the world, before they were
monks, and could not put off their cultivation of
mind or their learning with their secular dress;
and these would be the very men, in an age when
such talents were scarce, who would be taken out
of their retirement by superior authority, and who
therefore cannot fairly be quoted as ordinary
specimens of the monastic life.

Exceptio probat regulam : let us see what two

Doctors of the Church, one Greek, one Latin, both
rulers, both monks, say concerning the state, which
they at one time enjoyed, and afterwards lost.
" You tell me," says St Basil, writing to a friend
from his solitude, " that it was little for me to
describe the place of my retirement, unless I mentioned also my habits and my mode of life; yet
really I am ashamed to tell you how I pass night
and day in this lonely nook. I am like one who is
angry with the size of his vessel, as tossing over-
much, and leaves it for the boat, and is sea-sick
and miserable still. However, what I propose to
do is as follows, with the hope of tracing His steps
who has said, ' If any one will come after Me, let
him deny himself.' We must strive after a quiet
mind. As well might the eye ascertain an object
which is before it, while it roves up and down
without looking steadily at it, as a mind, distracted
with a thousand worldly cares, be able clearly to
apprehend the truth. One who is not yoked in
matrimony, is harassed by rebellious impulses and
hopeless attachments; he who is married, is involved in his own tumult of cares: is he without
children? he covets them; has he children? he
has anxieties about their education. Then there
is solicitude about his life, care of his house, over-
sight of his servants, misfortunes in trade, differ-
ences with his neighbours, lawsuits, the merchant's
risks, the farmer's toil. Each day, as it comes,
darkens the soul in its own way; and night after
night takes up the day's anxieties, and cheats us

with corresponding dreams. Now, the only way
of escaping all this is separation from the whole
world, so as to live without city, home, goods,
society, possessions, means of life, business, engagements, secular learning, that the heart may be
prepared as wax for the impress of divine teaching.
Solitude is of the greatest use for this purpose, as it
stills our passions, and enables reason to extirpate
them. Let then a place be found, such as mine,
separate from intercourse with men, that the tenor
of our exercises be not interrupted from without.
Pious exercises nourish the soul with divine
thoughts. Soothing hymns compose the mind to
a cheerful and calm state. Quiet, then, as I have
said, is the first step in our sanctification; the
tongue purified from the gossip of the world, the
eyes unexcited by fair colour or comely shape, the
ear secured from the relaxation of voluptuous songs,
and that especial mischief, light jesting. Thus,
the mind, rescued from dissipation from without,
and sensible allurements, falls back upon itself,
and thence ascends to the contemplation of God."
It is quite clear that at least St Basil took the same
view of the monastic state as we have done.

So much for the East in the fourth century; now
for the West in the seventh. "One day," says
St Gregory, after he had been constrained, against
his own wish, to leave his cloister for the government of the Universal Church, "one day, when I
was oppressed with the excessive trouble of secular
affairs, I sought a retired place, friendly to grief,

where whatever displeased me in my occupations
might show itself, and all that was wont to inflict
pain might be seen at one view." While he was
in this retreat, his most dear son, Peter, with
whom, since the latter was a youth, he had been
intimate, surprised him, and he opened his grief
to him. "My sad mind," he said, "labouring
under the soreness of its engagements, remembers
how it went with me formerly in this monastery,
how all perishable things were beneath it, how it
rose above all that was transitory, and, though
still in the flesh, went out in contemplation beyond
that prison, so that it even loved death, which is
commonly thought a punishment, as the gate of life
and the reward of labour. But now, in consequence of the pastoral charge, it undergoes the
busy work of secular men, and for that fair beauty
of its quiet, is dishonoured with the dust of the
earth. And often dissipating itself in outward
things, to serve the many, even when it seeks what
is inward, it comes home indeed, but is no longer
what it used to be." Here is the very same view
of the monastic state at Rome, which St Basil
had in Pontus—viz., retirement and repose. There
have been great Religious Orders since, whose
atmosphere has been conflict, and who have
thriven in smiting or in being smitten. It has
been their high calling; it has been their peculiar
meritorious service; but, as for the Benedictine,
the very air he breathes is peace.

We have now said enough both to explain and to

vindicate the biographer of St Maurus, when he says that the object, and life, and reward of the ancient monachism is " summa quies,"—the absence of all excitement, sensible and intellectual, and the vision of Eternity. And therefore have we called the monastic state the most poetical of religious disciplines. It was a return to that primitive age of the world, of which poets have so often sung, the simplicity of Arcadia or the reign of Saturn, when fraud and violence were unknown. It was a bringing-back of those real, not fabulous, scenes of innocence and miracle, when Adam delved, or Abel kept sheep, or Noe planted the vine, and Angels visited them. It was a fulfilment in the letter, of the glowing imagery of prophets, about the evangelical period. Nature for art, the wide earth and majestic heavens for the crowded city, the subdued and docile beasts of the field for the wild passions and rivalries of social life, tranquillity for ambition and care, divine meditation for the exploits of the intellect, the Creator for the creature, such was the normal condition of the monk. He had tried the world and found its hollowness; or he had eluded its fellowship, before it had solicited him;—and so St Antony fled to the desert, and St Hilarion sought the sea-shore, and St Basil ascended the mountain ravine, and St Benedict took refuge in his cave, and St Giles buried himself in the forest, and St Martin chose the broad river, in order that the world might be shut out of view, and the soul might be

at rest. And such a rest of intellect and of passion
as this is full of the elements of the poetical.

We have no intention of committing ourselves
here to a definition of poetry; we may be thought
wrong in the use of the term; but, if we explain
what we mean by it, no harm is done, whatever
be our inaccuracy, and each reader may substitute
for it some word he likes better. Poetry, then, we
conceive, whatever be its metaphysical essence, or
however various may be its kinds, whether it
more properly belongs to action or to suffering,
nay, whether it is more at home with society or
with nature, whether its spirit is seen to best
advantage in Homer or in Virgil, at any rate, is
always the antagonist to *science*. As science makes
progress in any subject-matter, poetry recedes from
it. The two cannot stand together; they belong
respectively to two modes of viewing things, which
are contradictory of each other. Reason investi-
gates, analyses, numbers, weighs, measures, ascer-
tains, locates, the objects of its contemplation,
and thus gains a scientific knowledge of them.
Science results in system, which is complex unity;
poetry delights in the indefinite and various as
contrasted with unity, and in the simple as contrasted with system. The aim of science is to get
a hold of things, to grasp them, to handle them,
to comprehend them; that is (to use the familiar
term), to *master* them, or to be superior to them.
Its success lies in being able to draw a line round
them, and to tell where each of them is to be found

within that circumference, and how each lies
relatively to all the rest. Its mission is to destroy
ignorance, doubt, surmise, suspense, illusions,
fears, deceits, according to the "Felix qui potuit
rerum cognoscere causas" of the Poet, whose
whole passage, by the way, may be taken as drawing out the contrast between the poetical and the
scientific. But as to the poetical, very different is
the frame of mind which is necessary for its perception. It demands, as its primary condition,
that we should not put ourselves above the objects
in which it resides, but at their feet; that we should
feel them to be above and beyond us, that we should
look up to them, and that, instead of fancying that
we can comprehend them, we should take for
granted that we are surrounded and comprehended
by them ourselves. It implies that we understand
them to be vast, immeasurable, impenetrable,
inscrutable, mysterious; so that at best we are
only forming conjectures about them, not conclusions, for the phenomena which they present
admit of many explanations, and we cannot know
the true one. Poetry does not address the reason,
but the imagination and affections; it leads to
admiration, enthusiasm, devotion, love. The
vague, the uncertain, the irregular, the sudden, are
among its attributes or sources. Hence it is that
a child's mind is so full of poetry, because he knows
so little; and an old man of the world so devoid
of poetry, because his experience of facts is so wide.
Hence it is that nature is commonly more poetical

than art, in spite of Lord Byron, because it is less comprehensible and less patient of definitions; history more poetical than philosophy; the savage than the citizen; the knight-errant than the brigadier-general; the winding bridle-path than the straight railroad; the sailing vessel than the steamer; the ruin than the spruce suburban box; the Turkish robe or Spanish doublet than the French dress coat. We have said far more than enough to make it clear what we mean by that element in the old monastic life, to which we have given the name of the Poetical.

Now, in many ways the family of St Benedict answers to this description, as we shall see if we look into its history. Its spirit indeed is ever one, but not its outward circumstances. It is not an Order proceeding from one mind at a particular date, and appearing all at once in its full per-fection, and in its extreme development, and in form one and the same everywhere, and from first to last, as is the case with other great religious institutions; but it is an organisation, diverse, complex, and irregular, and variously ramified, rich rather than symmetrical, with many origins and centres and new beginnings and the action of local influences, like some great natural growth; with tokens, on the face of it, of its being a divine work, not the mere creation of human genius. Instead of progressing on plan and system and from the will of a superior, it has shot forth and run out as if spontaneously, and has shaped itself according to events, from an irrepressible fulness of life within, and from the energetic self-action of its parts, like those symbolical creatures in the prophet's vision, which " went every one of them straight forward, whither the impulse of the spirit was to go." It has been poured out over the earth, rather than been sent, with a silent, mysterious operation, while men slept, and through the romantic adventures of individuals, which are well-nigh without record; and thus it has come down to us, not risen up among us, and is found rather than established. Its separate and scattered monasteries occupy the land, each in its place, with a majesty parallel, but superior, to that of old aristocratic houses. Their known antiquity, their unknown origin, their long eventful history, their connection with Saints and Doctors when on earth, the legends which hang about them, their rival ancestral honours, their extended sway, per-haps, over other religious houses, their hold upon the associations of the neighbourhood, their traditional friendships and compacts with other great landlords, the benefits they have conferred, the sanctity which they breathe, these and the like attributes make them objects at once of awe and of affection.

Such is the great Abbey of Bobio, in the Apen-nines, where St Columban came to die, having issued with his twelve monks from his convent in Benchor, county Down, and having spent his life in preaching godliness and planting monasteries

in half-heathen France and Burgundy. Such St
Gall's, on the lake of Constance, so called from
another Irishman, one of St Columban's companions, who remained in Switzerland, when his
master went on into Italy. Such the Abbey of
Fulda, where lies St Boniface, who, burning with
zeal for the conversion of the Germans, attempted
them a first time and failed, and then a second time
and succeeded, and at length crowned the missionary labours of forty-five years with martyrdom.
Such Monte Cassino, the metropolis of the Benedictine name, where the Saint broke the idol, and
cut down the grove, of Apollo. Ancient houses
such as these subdue the mind by the mingled
grandeur and sweetness of their presence. They
stand in history with an accumulated interest upon
them, which belongs to no other monuments of the
past. Whatever there is of venerable authority in
other foundations, in Bishops' sees, in Cathedrals,
in Colleges, respectively, is found in combination
in them. Each gate and cloister has had its own
story, and time has engraven upon their walls the
chronicle of its revolutions. And, even when at
length rudely destroyed, or crumbled into dust,
they live in history and antiquarian works, in the
pictures and relics which remain of them, and in
the traditions of their place.

In the early part of last century the Maurist
Fathers, with a view of collecting materials for the
celebrated works which they had then on hand,
sent two of their number on a tour through France

and the adjacent provinces.   Among other districts
the travellers passed through the forest of Ardennes,
which has been made classical by the prose of Cæsar
and the poetry of Shakespeare.   There they found
the great Benedictine Convent of St Hubert; and,
if we dwell a while upon the illustration which it
affords of what we have been saying, it is not as if
twenty other religious houses which they visited
would not serve our purpose quite as well, but
because it has come first to our hand in turning
over the pages of their volume.   At that time the
venerable abbey in question had upon it the weight
of a thousand years, and was eminent above others
in the country in wealth, in privileges, in name,
and, not the least recommendation, in the sanctity
of its members.   The lands, on which it was situated, were its freehold, and their range included
sixteen villages.   The old chronicle informs us
that, about the middle of the seventh century,
St Sigibert, the Merovingian, pitched upon
Ardennes and its neighbourhood for the establish-
ment of as many as twelve monasteries, with the
hope of thereby obtaining from heaven an heir to his
crown.   Dying prematurely, he but partially fulfilled his pious intention, which was taken up by
Pepin, sixty years afterwards, at the instance of
his chaplain, St Beregise; so far, at least, as to
make a commencement of the abbey of which we
are speaking.   Beregise had been a monk of the
Benedictine Abbey of St Tron, and he chose for its
site a spot in the midst of the forest, marked by the

ruins of a temple dedicated to the pagan Diana, the goddess of the chase. The holy man exorcised the place with the sign of the Cross; and, becoming abbot of the new house, filled it either with monks, or as seems less likely, with secular canons. From that time to the summer day when the two Maurists visited it, the sacred foundation, with various fortunes, had been in possession of the land.

On entering its precincts, they found it at once full and empty: empty of the monks, who were in the fields gathering in the harvest; full of pilgrims, who were wont to come day after day, in never-failing succession, to visit the tomb of St Hubert. What a series of events has to be recorded to make this simple account intelligible! and how poetical is the picture which it sets before us, as well as those events themselves, which it presupposes, when they come to be detailed! Were it not that we should be swelling a passing illustration into a history, we might go on to tell how strict the observance of the monks had been for the last hundred years before the travellers arrived there, since Abbot Nicholas de Fanson had effected a reform on the pattern of the French Congregation of St Vanne. We might relate how, when a simple monk in the Abbey of St Hubert, Nicholas had wished to change it for a stricter community, and how he got leave to go off to the Congregation just mentioned, and how then his old Abbot died suddenly, and how he himself to his surprise was elected in his place. And we might tell how, when

his mitre was on his head, he set about reforming
the house which he had been on the point of quitting,
and how he introduced for that purpose two monks
of St Vanne; and how the Bishop of Liége, in
whose diocese he was, set himself against this holy
design, and how some of the old monks attempted
to poison him; and how, though he carried it into
effect, still he was not allowed to aggregate his
Abbey to the Congregation whose reform he had
adopted; and how his good example encouraged
the neighbouring abbeys to commence a reform
in themselves, which issued in an ecclesiastical
union of the Flemish Benedictines.

All this, however, would not have been more
than one passage, of course, in the adventures which
had befallen the abbey and its abbots in the course
of its history. It had had many seasons of decay
before the time of Nicholas de Fanson, and many
restorations, and from different quarters. None
of them was so famous or important as the reform
effected in the year 817, about a century after its
original foundation, when the secular canons were
put out, and the monks put in, at the instance of
the then Bishop of Liége, who had a better spirit
than his successor in the time of Nicholas. The
new inmates were joined by some persons of noble
birth from the Cathedral, and by their suggestion and influence the bold measure was taken of
attempting to gain from Liége the body of the great
St Hubert, the Apostle of Ardennes. Great, we
may be sure, was the resistance of the city where

he lay; but Abbot Alreus, the friend and fellow-
workman of St Benedict of Anian, the first Re-
former of the Order before the date of Cluni, went
to the Bishop, and he went to the Archbishop of
Cologne; and then both prelates went to the
Emperor Louis le Debonnaire, the son of Charlemagne, whose favourite hunting ground the forest
was; and he referred the matter to the great
Council of Aix-la-Chapelle, whence a decision came
in favour of the monks of Ardennes. So with
great solemnity the sacred body was conveyed by
water to its new destination; and there in the
Treasury, in memorial of the happy event, the
Maurist visitors saw the very chalice of gold, and
the beautiful copy of the Gospels, ornamented with
precious stones, given to the Abbey by Louis at
the time. Doubtless it was the handiwork of the
monks of some other Benedictine House, as must
have been the famous Psalter, of which the visitors
speak also, written in letters of gold, the gift of
Louis's son, the Emperor Lothaire; and there he
sits in the first page, with his crown on his head,
his sceptre in one hand, his sheathed sword in the
other, and something very like a fleur-de-lys
buckling on his ermine robe at the shoulder:—
which precious gift, that is, the Psalter with all its
pictures, two centuries after came most unaccount-
ably into the possession of the Lady Helvidia of
Aspurg, who gave it to her young son Bruno,
afterwards Pope Leo the Ninth, to learn the Psalms
by; but, as the young Saint made no progress in

his task, she came to the conclusion that she had no right to the book, and so she ended by making a pilgrimage to St Hubert with Bruno, and not only gave back the Psalter, but made the offering of a Sacramentary besides.

But to return to the relics of the Saint; the sacred body was taken by water up the Maes. The coffin was of marble, and perhaps could have been taken no other way; but another reason, besides its weight, lay in the indignation of the citizens of Liége, who made several attempts, in the following years, to regain the body. In consequence, the good monks of Ardennes hid it within the walls of their monastery, confiding the secret of its whereabouts to only two of their community at a time; and they showed in the sacristy to the devout, instead, the Saint's ivory cross and his stole, the sole of his shoe and his comb, and Diana, Marchioness of Autrech, gave a golden box to hold the stole. This, however, was in after times; for they were very loath at first to let strangers within their cloisters at all; and in 838, when a long spell of rain was destroying the crops, and the people of the neighbourhood came in procession to the shrine to ask the intercession of the Saint, the cautious Abbot Sewold, availing himself of the Rule, would only admit priests, and them by threes and fours, with naked feet, and a few laymen with each of them. The supplicants were good men, however, and had no notion of playing any trick; they came in piety and devotion, and the

D

rain ceased, and the country was the gainer by St Hubert of Ardennes. And thenceforth others, besides the monks, became interested in his stay in the forest.

And now we have said something in explanation why the courtyard was full of pilgrims, when the travellers came. St Hubert had been an object of devotion for a particular benefit, perhaps ever since he came there, certainly as early as the eleventh century, for we then have historical notice of it. His preference of the forest to the city, which he had shown in life before his conversion, was illustrated by the particular grace or miraculous service, for which, more than for any other, he used his glorious intercession on high. He is famous for curing those who had suffered from the bite of wild animals, especially dogs of the chase, and a hospital was attached to the Abbey for their reception. The sacristan of the Church officiated in the cure; and with rites which never indeed failed, but which to some cautious persons seemed to savour of superstition. Certainly they were startling at first sight; accordingly a formal charge on that score was at one time brought against them before the Bishop of Liége, and a process followed. The Bishop, the University of Louvain, and its Faculty of Medicine conducted the inquiry, which was given in favour of the Abbey, on the ground that what looked like a charm might be of the nature of a medical regimen.

However, though the sacristan was the medium

of the cure, the general care of the patients was left to externs. The hospital was served by secular priests, since the monks heard no confessions save those of their own people. This rule they observed, in order to reserve themselves to the proper duties of a Benedictine,—the choir, study, manual labour, and transcription of books; and, while the Maurists were ocular witnesses of their agricultural toils, they saw the diligence of their penmanship in its results, for the MSS. of their Library were the choicest in the country. Among them, they tell us, were copies of St Jerome's Bible, the Acts of the Councils, Bede's History, Gregory and Isidore, Origen and Augustine.

The Maurists report as favourably of the monastic buildings themselves as of the hospital and library. Those buildings were a chronicle of past times, and of the changes which had taken place in them. First there were the poor huts of St Beregise upon the half-cleared and still marshy ground of the forest; then came the rebuilding, when St Hubert was brought there; and centuries after that, St Thierry, the intimate friend of the great Pope Hildebrand, had renewed it magnificently, at the time that he was Abbot. He was sadly treated in his lifetime by his monks, as Nicholas after him; but, after his death, they found out that he was a Saint, which they might have discovered before it; and they placed him in the crypt, and there he and another holy Abbot after him lay in peace, till the Calvinists broke into it in the sixteenth

century, and burned both of them to ashes.   There
were marks too of the same fanatics on the pillars
of the nave of the church; which had been built
by Abbot John de Wahart in the twelfth century,
and then again from its foundations by Abbots
Nicholas de Malaise and Romaclus, the friend of
Blosius, four centuries later; and it was ornamented
by Abbot Cyprian, who was called the friend of
the poor; and doubtless the travellers admired
the marble of the choir and sanctuary, and the
silver candelabra of the altar given by the reigning
Lord Abbot; and perhaps they heard him sing
solemn Mass on the Assumption, as was usual on
that feast, with his four secular chaplains, one to
carry his Cross, another his mitre, a third his
gremial, and a fourth his candle, and accompanied
by the pealing organ and the many clattering bells,
which had been the gift of Abbot Balla about a
hundred years earlier.   Can we imagine a more
graceful union of human with divine, of the sweet
with the austere, of business and of calm, of
splendour and of simplicity, than is displayed in a
great religious house after this pattern, when un-
relaxed in its observance, and pursuing the ends
for which it was endowed?

The monks had been accused of choosing beautiful spots for their dwellings; as if this were a luxury
in ascetics, and not rather the necessary alleviation
of their penances.   Even when their critics are
kindest, they consider such sites as chosen by a
sort of sentimental, ornamental indolence.   "Beau-

lieu river," says Mr Warner in his topography of Hampshire, and, as he writes far less ill-naturedly than the run of authors, we will quote him, " Beaulieu river is stocked with plenty of fish, and boasts in particular of good oysters and fine plaice, and is fringed quite to the edge of the water with the most beautiful hanging woods. In the area enclosed are distinct traces of various fish-ponds, formed for the use of the convent. Some of them continue perfect to the present day, and abound with fish. A curious instance occurs also of monkish luxury, even in the article of water; to secure a fine spring those monastics have spared neither trouble nor expense. About half a mile to the south-east of the Abbey is a deep wood; and at a spot almost inaccessible is a cave formed of smooth stones. It has a very contracted entrance, but spreads gradually into a little apartment, of seven feet wide, ten deep, and about five high. This covers a copious and transparent spring of water, which, issuing from the mouth of the cave, is lost in a deep dell, and is there received, as I have been informed, by a chain of small stone pipes, which formerly, when perfect, conveyed it quite to the Abbey. It must be confessed, the monks in general displayed an elegant taste in the choice of their situations. Beaulieu Abbey is a striking proof of this. Perhaps few spots in the kingdom could have been pitched upon, better calculated for monastic seclusion than this. The deep woods, with which it is almost environed,

throw an air of gloom and solemnity over the scene,
well suited to excite religious emotions; while the
stream that glides by its side, afforded to the
recluse a striking emblem of human life: and at
the same time that it soothed his mind by a gentle
murmuring, led it to serious thought by its continual and irrevocable lesson."

The monks were not so soft as all this, after all;
and if Mr Warner had seen them, we feel sure he
would have been astonished at the stern, as well
as sweet simplicity which characterised them.
They were not dreamy sentimentalists, to fall in
love with melancholy winds and purling rills, and
waterfalls and nodding groves; but their poetry
was the poetry of hard work and hard fare, unselfish
hearts and charitable hands. They could plough
and reap, they could hedge and ditch, they could
drain; they could lop, they could carpenter; they
could thatch, they could make hurdles for their
huts; they could make a road, they could divert
or secure the streamlet's bed, they could bridge a
torrent. Mr Warner mentions one of their luxuries,
—clear, wholesome water; it was an allowable one,
especially as they obtained it by their own patient
labour. If their grounds are picturesque, if their
views are rich, they made them so, and had, we
presume, a right to enjoy the work of their own
hands. They found a swamp, a moor, a thicket,
a rock, and they made an Eden in the wilderness.
They destroyed snakes; they extirpated wild cats,
wolves, boars, bears; they put to flight or they

converted rovers, outlaws, robbers. The gloom
of the forest departed, and the sun, for the first
time since the Deluge, shone upon the moist ground.
St Benedict is the true man of Ross.

" Who hung with woods yon mountain's sultry
    brow?
  From the dry rock who made the waters flow?
  Whose causeway parts the vale with shady rows?
  Whose seats the weary traveller repose?
  He feeds yon almshouse, neat, but void of state,
  When Age and Want sit smiling at the gate;
  Him portioned maids, apprenticed orphans
    blessed,
  The young who labour, and the old who rest."

And candid writers, though not Catholics, allow it.
Even English, and much more foreign historians
and antiquarians, have arrived at a unanimous
verdict here. " We owe the agricultural restoration of great part of Europe to the monks," says Mr
Hallam. "The monks were much the best husbandmen, and the only gardeners," says Forsyth.
" None," says Wharton, " ever improved their
lands and possessions more than the monks, by
building, cultivating, and other methods." The
cultivation of Church lands, as Sharon Turner infers
from Doomsday Book, was superior to that held
by other proprietors, for there was less wood upon
them, less common pasture, and more abundant
meadow. " Wherever they came," says Mr Soame
on Mosheim, " they converted the wilderness into a
cultivated country; they pursued the breeding

of cattle and agriculture, laboured with their own hands, drained morasses, and cleared away forests. By them Germany was rendered a fruitful country." M. Guizot speaks as strongly: "The Benedictine monks were the agriculturalists of Europe; they cleared it on a large scale, associating agriculture with preaching."

St Benedict's direct object in setting his monks to manual labour, was neither social usefulness nor poetry, but penance; still his work was both the one and the other. The above-cited authors enlarge upon its use, and we may be allowed to dwell upon its poetry; we may contemplate both its utility to man and its service to God in the aspect of its poetry. How romantic then, as well as useful, how lively as well as serious, is their history, with its episodes of personal adventure and prowess, its pictures of squatter, hunter, farmer, civil engineer, and evangelist united in the same individual, its supernatural colouring of heroic virtue and miracle! When St Columban first came into Burgundy with his twelve young monks, he placed himself in a vast wilderness, and made them set about cultivating the soil. At first they all suffered from hunger, and were compelled to live on the barks of trees and wild herbs. On one occasion they were for five days in this condition. St Gall, one of them, betook himself to a Swiss forest, fearful from the multitude of wild beasts; and then, choosing the neighbourhood of a mountain stream, he made a cross of twigs, and hung some relics on it, and laid the foundation of his celebrated abbey. St Ronan came from Ireland to Cornwall, and chose a wood, full of wild beasts, for his hermitage, near the Lizard. The monks of St Dubritius, the founder of the Welsh schools, also sought the woods, and there they worked hard at manufactures, agriculture, and road-making. St Sequanus placed himself where "the trees almost touched the clouds." He and his companions, when they first explored it, asked themselves how they could penetrate into it, when they saw a winding footpath, so narrow and full of briars, that it was with difficulty that one foot followed another. With much labour and with torn clothes they succeeded in gaining its depths, and stooping their heads into the darkness at their feet, they perceived a cavern, shrouded by the thick interlacing branches of the trees, and blocked up with stones and underwood. "This," says the monastic account, "was the cavern of robbers, and the resort of evil spirits." Sequanus fell on his knees, prayed, made the sign of the Cross over the abyss, and built his cell there. Such was the first foundation of the celebrated abbey called after him in Burgundy.

Sturm, the Bavarian convert of St Boniface, was seized with a desire, as his master had been in his English monastery, of founding a religious house in the wilds of pagan Germany; and setting out with two companions, he wandered for two days through the Buchonian forest, and saw nothing but earth, sky, and large trees. On the third day he stopped and chose a spot, which on trial did not answer. Then, mounting an ass, he set out by himself, cutting down branches of a night to secure himself from the wild beasts, till at length he came to the place (described by St Boniface as "locum silvaticum in eremo, vastissimæ solitudinis"), in which afterwards rose the abbey and schools of Fulda. Wunibald was suspicious of the good wine of the Rhine where he was, and, determining to leave it, he bought the land where Heidensheim afterwards stood, then a wilderness of trees and underwood, covering a deep valley and the sides of lofty mountains. There he proceeded, axe in hand, to clear the ground for his religious house, while the savage natives looked on sullenly, jealous for their hunting grounds and sacred trees. Willibald, his brother, had pursued a similar work on system; he had penetrated his forest in every direction and scattered monasteries over it. The Irish Alto pitched himself in a wood, half way between Munich and Vienna. Pirminius chose an island, notorious for its snakes, and there he planted his hermitage and chapel, which at length became the rich and noble abbey and school of Augia Major or Richenau.

The more celebrated School of Bec had a similar beginning at a later date, when Herluin, an old soldier, devoted his house and farm to an ecclesiastical purpose, and governed, as abbot, the monastery which he had founded. "You might see him," says the writer of his life, " when office was over in church, going out to his fields, at the head of his monks, with his bag of seed about his neck, and his rake or hoe in his hand. There he remained with them hard at work till the day was closing. Some were employed in clearing the land of brambles and weeds; others spread manure; others were weeding or sowing; no one ate his bread in idleness. Then when the hour came for saying office in church, they all assembled together punctually. Their ordinary food was bread of bran, and vegetables with salt and water; and the water muddy, for the well was two miles off." Lanfranc, then a secular, was so overcome by the simple Abbot, fresh from the field, setting about his baking with dirty hands, that he forthwith became one of the party; and being unfitted for labour, opened in the house a school of logic, thereby to make money for the community. Such was the cradle of the scholastic theology; the last years of the patristic, which were nearly contemporaneous, exhibit a similar scene:—St Bernard founding his abbey of Clairvaux in a place called the Valley of Wormwood, in the heart of a savage forest, the haunt of robbers, and his thirteen companions grubbing up a homestead, raising a few huts, and living on barley or cockle bread with boiled beech leaves for vegetables.

How beautiful is Simeon of Durham's account of Easterwine, the first abbot after Bennet of St Peter's at Wearmouth! He was a man of noble

birth, who gave himself to religion, and died young.
"Though he had been in the service of King
Egfrid," says Simeon, "when he had once left
secular affairs, and laid aside his arms, and taken
on him the spiritual warfare instead, he was nothing
but the humble monk, just like any of his brethren,
winnowing with them with great joy, milking the
ewes and cows, and in the bakehouse, the garden,
the kitchen, and all house duties, cheerful and
obedient. And, when he received the name of
Abbot, still he was in spirit just what he was
before to every one, gentle, affable, and kind; or,
if any fault had been committed, correcting it
indeed by the Rule, but still so winning the offender
by his unaffected earnest manner, that he had no
wish ever to repeat the offence, or to dim the bright-
ness of that most clear countenance with the cloud
of his transgression. And often going here and
there on business of the monastery, when he found
his brothers at work, he would at once take part
in it, guiding the plough, or shaping the iron, or
taking the winnowing fan, or the like. He was
young and strong, with a sweet voice, a cheerful
temper, a liberal heart, and a handsome countenance. He partook of the same food as his
brethren, and under the same roof. He slept in
the common dormitory, as before he was abbot, and
he continued to do so for the first two days of his ill-
ness, when death had now seized him, as he knew full
well. But for the last five days he betook himself
to a more retired dwelling; and then, coming out

into the open air and sitting down, and calling for all his brethren, after the manner of his tender nature, he gave his weeping monks the kiss of peace, and died at night while they were singing lauds."

This gentleness and tenderness of heart seems to have been as characteristic of the monks as their simplicity; and if there are some Saints among them who on the public stage of history do not show it, it was because they were called out of their convents for some special purpose. Bede goes out of his way to observe of Ethelbert, on St Austin's converting him, that "he had learned from the teachers and authors of his salvation, that men were to be drawn heavenwards, and not forced." Aldhelm, when a council had been held about the perverse opinions of the British Christians, seconding the principle which the Fathers of it laid down, that "schismatics were to be convinced, not compelled," wrote a book upon their error and converted many of them. Wolstan, when the civil power failed in its attempts to stop the slave-trade of the Bristol people, succeeded by his persevering preaching. In the confessional he was so gentle, that penitents came to him from all parts of England. This has been the spirit of the monks from the first. The student of ecclesiastical history may recollect a certain passage in St Martin's history, when his desire to shield the Spanish heretics from death brought him into difficulties, from which he hardly escaped, in his mode of dealing with the usurper Maximus.

Penance indeed and mercy have gone hand in hand in the history of the monks; from the Solitaries in Egypt down to the Trappists of this day, it is one of the points in which the unity of the monastic idea shows itself. They have ever toiled for others, while they toiled for themselves; nor for posterity only, but for their poor neighbours, and for travellers who came to them. St Augustine tells us, that the monks of Egypt and of the East made so much by manual labour as to be able to freight vessels with provisions for impoverished districts. Theodoret speaks of a certain five thousand of them, who by their labour supported, besides themselves, innumerable poor and strangers. Sozomen speaks of the monk Zeno, who, though a hundred years old, and the bishop of a rich Church, worked for the poor as well as for himself. Corbinian in a subsequent century surrounded his German Church with fruit trees and vines, and sustained the poor with the produce. The monks of St Gall, already mentioned, gardened, planted, fished, and thus secured the means of relieving the poor and entertaining strangers. "Monasteries," says Neander, "were seats for the promotion of various trades, arts, and sciences. The gains accruing from their combined labour were employed for the relief of the distressed. In great famines, thousands were rescued from starvation." In a scarcity at the beginning of the twelfth century, a monastery in the neighbourhood of Cologne distributed in one day fifteen hundred alms, consisting of bread, meat, and vegetables. About the same time, St Bernard founded his monastery of Cîteaux, which, though situated in the waste district described above, was able at length to sustain two thousand poor for months, besides extraordinary alms bestowed on others. The monks offered their simple hospitality, un-inviting as it might be, to high as well as low; and to those who scorned their fare, they at least could offer a refuge in misfortune or danger, or after casualties.

Duke William, ancestor of the Conqueror, was hunting in the woods about Jumieges, when he fell in with a rude hermitage. Two monks had made their way through the forest, and with immense labour had rooted up some trees, levelled the ground, raised some crops, and put together their hut. William heard their story, not perhaps in the best humour, and flung aside in contempt the barley bread and water which they offered him. Presently he was brought back wounded and insensible: he had got the worst in an en-counter with a boar. On coming to himself, he accepted the hospitality which he had refused at first, and built for them a monastery. Doubtless he had looked on them as trespassers or squatters on his domain, though with a religious character and object. The Norman princes were as good friends to the wild beasts as the monks were enemies: a charter still exists of the Conqueror granted to the abbey of Caen, in which he stipulates that its inmates should not turn the woods into tillage, and reserves the game for himself.

Contrast with this savage retreat and its rude hospitality, the different, though equally Benedictine picture of the sacred grove of Subiaco, and the spiritual entertainment which it ministers to all comers, as given in the late pilgrimage of Bishop Ullathorne: " The trees," he says, " which form the venerable grove, are very old, but their old age is vigorous and healthy. Their great gray roots expose themselves to view with all manner of curling lines and wrinkles on them, and the rough stems bend and twine about with the vigour and ease of gigantic pythons. . . . Of how many holy solitaries have these trees witnessed the meditations! And then they have seen beneath their quiet boughs the irruption of mailed men, tormented by the thirst of plunder and the passion of blood, which even a sanctuary held so sacred could not stay. And then they have witnessed, for twelve centuries and more, the greatest of the Popes, the Gregories, the Leos, the Innocents, and the Piuses, coming one after another to refresh themselves from their labours in a solitude which is steeped with the inspirations and redolent with the holiness of St Benedict."

What congenial subjects for his verse would the sweetest of all poets have found in scenes and histories such as the foregoing, he who in his Georgics has shown such love of a country life and country occupations, and of the themes and trains of thought which rise out of the country! Would that Christianity had a Virgil to describe the old monks at their rural labours, as it has had a Sacchi or a Domenichino to paint them! How would he have been able to set forth the adventures and the hardships of the missionary husbandmen, who sang of the Scythian winter, and the murrain of the cattle, the stag of Sylvia, and the forest home of Evander! How could he have portrayed St Paulinus or St Serenus in his garden, who could draw so beautiful a picture of the old Corycian, raising amid the thicket his scanty potherbs upon the nook of land, which was "not good for tillage, nor for pasture, nor for vines"! How could he have brought out the poetry of those simple labourers, who has told us of that old man's flowers and fruits, and of the satisfaction, as a king's, which he felt in those innocent riches! He who had so huge a dislike of cities, and great houses, and high society, and sumptuous banquets, and the canvass for office, and the hard law, and the noisy lawyer, and the statesman's harangue,—he who thought the country proprietor as even too blessed, did he but know his blessedness, and who loved the valley, winding stream, and wood, and the hidden life which they offer, and the deep lessons which they whisper,—how could he have illustrated that wonderful union of prayer, penance, toil, and literary work, the true "otium cum dignitate," a fruitful leisure and a meek-hearted dignity, which

E

is exemplified in the Benedictine! That ethereal
fire which enabled the prince of Latin poets to take
up the Sibyl's strain, and to adumbrate the glories
of a supernatural future, that serene philosophy,
which has strewn his poems with sentiments which
come home to the heart, that intimate sympathy
with the sorrows of human kind and with the action
and passion of human nature, how well would they
have served to illustrate the patriarchal history and
office of the monks in the broad German countries,
or the deeds, the words, and the visions of a St
Odilo or a St Aelred!

What a poet deliberately chooses for the subject
of his poems, must be in its own nature poetical.
A poet indeed is but a man after all, and in his
proper person may prefer solid beef and pudding
to all the creations of his own "fine frenzy,"
which, in his character of poet, are his meat and
drink. But no poet will ever commit his poetical
reputation to the treatment of subjects which do
not admit of poetry. When, then, Virgil chooses
the country and rejects the town, he shows us
that a certain aspect of the town is uncongenial
with poetry, and that a certain aspect of the
country is congenial. Repose, intellectual and
moral, is that quality of country life which he
selects for his praises; and effort, and bustle, and
excitement is that quality of town life which he
abhors. Herein then, according to Virgil, lies the
poetry of St Benedict, in the "secura quies et
nescia fallere vita," in the absence of anxiety and

fretfulness, of schemes and scheming, of hopes and
fears, of doubts and disappointments.   Such a life,
—living for the day without solicitude for the
morrow, without plans or objects, even holy ones,
here below; working, not (so to say) by the piece,
but as hired by the hour; sowing the ground with
the certainty, according to the promise, of reaping;
reading or writing this present week without the
consequent necessity of reading or writing during
the next; dwelling among one's own people without distant ties; taking each new day as a whole
in itself, an addition, not a complement, to the past;
and doing works which cannot be cut short, for
they are complete in every portion of them,—such
a life may be called emphatically Virgilian.   They,
on the contrary, whose duty lies in what may be
called *undertakings*, in science and system, in sustained efforts of the intellect or elaborate processes
of action,—apologists, controversialists, disputants
in the schools, professors in the chair, teachers in
the pulpit, rulers in the Church,—have a noble and
meritorious mission, but not so poetical a one.
When the bodily frame receives an injury, or is
seized with some sudden malady, nature may be
expected to set right the evil, if left to itself, but
she requires time; science comes in to shorten
the process, and is violent that it may be certain.
This may be taken to illustrate St Benedict's mode
of counteracting the miseries of life.   He found the
world, physical and social, in ruins, and his mission
was to restore it in the way, not of science, but of

nature, not as if setting about to do it, not professing to do it by any set time or by any rare specific or by any series of strokes, but so quietly, patiently, gradually, that often, till the work was done, it was not known to be doing. It was a restoration, rather than a visitation, correction, or conversion. The new world which he helped to create was a growth rather than a structure. Silent men were observed about the country, or discovered in the forest, digging, clearing, and building; and other silent men, not seen, were sitting in the cold cloister, tiring their eyes, and keeping their attention on the stretch, while they painfully deciphered and copied and re-copied the manuscripts which they had saved. There was no one that "contended, or cried out," or drew attention to what was going on; but by degrees the woody swamp became a hermitage, a religious house, a farm, an abbey, a village, a seminary, a school of learning, and a city. Roads and bridges connected it with other abbeys and cities, which had similarly grown up; and what the haughty Alaric or fierce Attila had broken to pieces, these patient meditative men had brought together and made to live again.

And then, when they had in the course of many years gained their peaceful victories, perhaps some new invader came, and with fire and sword undid their slow and persevering toil in an hour. The Hun succeeded to the Goth, the Lombard to the Hun, the Tartar to the Lombard; the Saxon was reclaimed only that the Dane might take his place.

Down in the dust lay the labour and civilisation of
centuries,—Churches, Colleges, Cloisters, Libraries,
—and nothing was left to them but to begin over
again; but this they did without grudging, so
promptly, cheerfully, and tranquilly, as if it were
by some law of nature that the restoration came,
and they were like the flowers and shrubs and fruit
trees which they reared, and which, when ill-treated,
do not take vengeance, or remember evil, but give
forth fresh branches, leaves, or blossoms, perhaps
in greater profusion, or with richer quality, for the
very reason that the old were rudely broken off.
If one holy place was desecrated, the monks
pitched upon another, and by this time there were
rich or powerful men who remembered and loved
the past enough, to wish to have it restored in the
future.   Thus was it in the case of the monastery
of Ramsey after the ravages of the Danes.   A
wealthy Earl, whose heart was touched, consulted
his Bishop how he could best promote the divine
glory: the Bishop answered that they only were
free, serene, and unsolicitous, who renounced the
world, and that their renunciation brought a
blessing on their country. "By their merit," he
said, "the anger of the Supreme Judge is abated;
a healthier atmosphere is granted; corn springs
up more abundantly; famine and pestilence with-
draw; the state is better governed; prisons are
opened; the fetters unbound; the shipwrecked
relieved." He proceeded to advise him as to the
best of courses, to give ground for a monastery, and

to build and endow it.   Earl Alwin observed in
reply, that he had inherited some waste land in the
midst of marshes, with a forest in the neighbourhood, some open spots of good turf, and others of
meadow; and he took the Bishop to see it.   It
was in fact an island in the fens, and as lonely as
religious men could desire.   The gift was accepted,
workmen were collected, the pious peasants round
about gave their labour.   Twelve monks were
found from another cloister; cells and a chapel
were soon raised.   Materials were collected for a
handsome church; stones and cement were given;
a firm foundation was secured; scaffolding and
machinery were lent; and in course of time a
sacred edifice and two towers rose over the desolate
waste, and renewed the past;—a learned divine
from France was invited to preside over the
monastic school.

Here then we are led lastly to speak of the literary
labours of the Benedictines, but we have not room
to do more than direct attention to the peculiar
character of their work, and must pass over their
schools altogether.   Here, as in other respects,
above noticed, the unity of monachism shows itself.
What the Benedictines have been, even in their
latest literary developments, in St Maur in the
seventeenth century, and at Solesme now, such were
the monks in their first years.   One of the chief
occupations of the disciples of St Pachomius in
Egypt was the transcription of books.   It was the
sole labour of the monks of St Martin in Gaul.

The Syrian solitaries, according to St Chrysostom, employed themselves in making copies of the Holy Scriptures. It was the occupation of the monks of St Equitius and of Cassiodorus, and of the nunnery of St Cæsarius. We read of one holy man preparing the skins for writing, of another selling his manuscripts in order to gain alms for the poor, and of an abbess writing St Peter's Epistles in letters of gold. St David had shown the same reverence to St John's Gospel. Abbot Plato filled his own and other monasteries with his beautifully written volumes. During the short rule, of Abbot Desiderius at Monte Cassino, his monks wrote out St Austin's fifty Homilies, his Letters, his Comment upon the Sermon on the Mount, upon St Paul and upon Genesis; parts of St Jerome and St Ambrose, part of St Bede, St Leo's Sermons, the Orations of St Gregory Nazianzen; the Acts of the Apostles, the Epistles and the Apocalypse; various histories, including that of St Gregory of Tours, Josephus on the Jewish War, Justinian's Institutes, and many ascetic and other works; of the Classics, Cicero de Natura Deorum, Terence, Ovid's *Fasti*, Horace, and Virgil. Maurus Lapi, a Camaldolese, in the fifteenth century, copied a thousand volumes in less than fifty years. Jerome, a monk in an Austrian monastery, wrote so great a number of books, that, it is said, a waggon with six horses would scarcely suffice to draw them. Othlon, in the eleventh century, when a boy, wrote so diligently, that he

nearly lost his sight. That was in France; he
then went to Ratisbon, where he wrote nineteen
missals, three books of the Gospel, two books of
Epistle and Gospel, and many others. Many he
gave to his friends, but the list is too long to finish.
The Abbot Odo of Tournay "used to exult,"
according to his successor, "in the number of
writers which the Lord had given him. Had you
gone into his cloister, you might have seen a dozen
young men sitting in perfect silence, writing at
tables, constructed for the purpose. All Jerome's
Commentaries on the Prophets, all the works of
St Gregory, all that he could find of Austin,
Ambrose, Isidore, Bede, and the Lord Anselm,
Abbot of Bec, and afterwards Archbishop of Canterbury, he caused to be diligently transcribed."

These tranquil labourers found a further field
in the illumination and binding of the transcribed
volumes, as they had previously been occupied in
the practice necessary for the then important art
of caligraphy. It was not running hand that the
monks had to learn; for it was no ephemeral expression of their own thoughts which their writing
was to convey, but the formal transcript, for the
benefit of posterity, of the words of inspired teachers
and Doctors of the Church. They were performing
what has been since the printer's work; and it is
said that from the English monks is derived the
small letter of the modern Roman type. In France
the abbeys of Fontenelle, Rheims, and Corbie were
especially famed for beauty of penmanship in the

age of Charlemagne, when literature was in its
most depressed state.   Books intended for presents,
such as that which the mother of Leo the Ninth
presented to St Hubert, and, much more, if intended
for sacred uses, were enriched with gold and silver
plates and precious stones.   Here was a commencement of the cultivation of the fine arts in those
turbulent times,—a quiet, unexciting occupation,
which went on inside the monasteries, whatever
rivalries or heresies agitated Christendom outside
of them, and which, though involving, of course,
an improvement in the workmanship as time went
on, yet in the case of every successive specimen,
whatever exact degree of skill or taste each exhibited, had its end in itself, as though there had
been no other specimen before or after.

Brower, in his work on the *Antiquities of Fulda*,
gives us a lively picture of the various tranquil
occupations, which were going on at one time
within the monastic walls.   "As industrious
bees," he says, "their work never flagging, did
these monks follow out their calling.   Some of them
were engaged in describing, here and there upon
the parchment, the special letters and characters
which were to be filled in; others were wrapping
or binding the manuscripts in handsome covers;
others were marking out in red the remarkable
sentences or the heads of the chapters.   Some were
writing fairly what had been thrown together at
random, or had been left out in the dictation, and
were putting every part in fair order.   And not a

few of them excelled in painting in all manner of colours, and in drawing figures." He goes on to refer to an old manuscript there which speaks of the monks as decorating their church, and of their carpenters' work, sculpture, engraving, and brass work.

We have mentioned St Dunstan in an earlier page as called to political duties, which were out of keeping with the traditionary spirit of his Order; here, however, he shows himself in the simple character of a Benedictine. He had a taste for the arts generally, especially music. He painted and embroidered; his skill in smith's work is recorded in the well-known legend of his combat with the evil one. And, as the monks of Hilarion joined gardening with psalmody, and Bernard and his Cistercians joined field work with meditation, so did St Dunstan use music and painting as directly expressive or suggestive of devotion. "He excelled in writing, painting, moulding in wax, carving in wood and bone, and in work in gold, silver, iron, and brass," says the writer of his life in Surius. "And he used his skill in musical instruments, to charm away himself and others from secular annoyances, and to rouse them to the thought of heavenly harmony, both by the sweet words with which he accompanied his airs, and by the concord of those airs themselves." And then he goes on to mention, how on one occasion, when he had hung his harp against the wall, and the wind brought out from its strings a wild melody, he recognised in it one of the antiphons in the Commune Martyrum, " Gaudete in Cœlis," etc., and used it for his own humiliation.

As might be expected, the monasteries of the South of Europe would not be behind the North in accomplishments of this kind. Those of St Gall, Monte Cassino, and Solignac are especially spoken of as skilled in the fine arts. Monte Cassino excelled in *miniatura* and mosaic, the Camaldolese in painting, and the Olivetans in wood-inlaying.

While manual labour, applied to these artistic purposes, ministered to devotion, on the other hand, when applied to the transcription and multiplication of books, it was a method of instruction, and that peculiarly Benedictine, as being of a literary, not a scientific nature. Systematic theology had but a limited place in ecclesiastical study prior to the eleventh and twelfth centuries; Scripture and the Fathers were the received means of education, and these constituted the very text on which the pens of the monks were employed. And thus they would be becoming familiar with that kind of knowledge which was proper to their vocation, at the same time that they were engaged in what was unequivocally a manual labour; and in providing for the religious necessities of posterity, they were directly serving their own edification. And this again had been the practice of the monks from the first, and is included in the *unity* of their profession. St Chrysostom tells us that their ordinary occupation in his time was " to sing and pray, to read Scripture, and to transcribe the sacred text." As the writings of the Fathers gradually became the literary property of the Church, these, too, became the subject-matter of the reading and the writing of the monks. " For him who is going on to perfection," says St Benedict in his Rule, " there are the lessons of the Holy Fathers, which lead to its very summit. For what page, what passage of the Old or New Testament, coming as it does with divine authority, is not the very exactest rule of life? What book of the Holy Catholic Fathers does not resound with this one theme, how we may take the shortest course to our Creator? " But we need not here insist on this characteristic of monastic study, which, especially as regards the study of Scripture, has been treated so fully and so well by Mr Maitland in his *Essays on the Dark Ages*.

The sacred literature of the monks went a step farther. They would be naturally led by their continual perusal of the Scriptures and the Fathers, to attempt to compare and adjust these two chief sources of theological truth with each other. Hence resulted the peculiar character of the religious works of what may be especially called the Benedictine period, the five centuries between St Gregory and St Anselm. The age of the fathers was well-nigh over; the age of the schoolmen was yet to come; the ecclesiastical writers of the intervening period employed themselves for the most part in arranging and digesting the patristical literature

which had come down to them; they either strung
together choice passages of the Fathers in *catenæ*
as a running illustration of the inspired text, or
they formed them into a comment upon it. The
Summæ Sententiarum of the same period were works
of a similar character, while they also opened the
way to the intellectual exercises of the scholastic
period; for they were lessons or instructions
arranged according to a scheme or system of doctrine, though they were still extracted from the
works of the Fathers, and though the matter of
those works suggested the divisions or details of
the system. Moreover, such labours, as much as
transcription itself, were Benedictine in their spirit,
as well as in their subject-matter; for where there
was nothing of original research, nothing of brilliant
or imposing result, there would be nothing to
dissipate, elate, or absorb the mind, or to violate
the simplicity and tranquillity proper to the
monastic state.

The same remark applies to a further literary
employment in which the Benedictines allowed
themselves, and which is the last we shall here
mention, and that is the compilation of chronicles
and annals, whether ecclesiastical, secular, or
monastic. So prominent a place does this take in
their literature, that the author of the *Asceticon*,
in the fourth volume of Dom François's " Biblio-
thèque des Écrivains Bénédictins," does not hesi-
tate to point to the historical writings of his
Order as constituting one of its chief claims, after

its Biblical works, on the gratitude of posterity.
"This," he says, "is the praise especially due to
the monks, that they have illustrated Holy Scripture, rescued history, sacred and profane, from the
barbarism of the times, and have handed down to
posterity so many lives both of Saints and of
Bishops." Here again is a fresh illustration of the
Benedictine character; for first, those histories are
of the most simple structure and most artless
composition, and next, from the circumstance of
their being commonly narratives of contemporary
events, or compilations from a few definite sources
of information which were at hand, they involved
nothing of that laborious research and excitement
of mind which is demanded of the writer who has
to record a complex course of history, extending
over many centuries and countries, and who aims
at the discovery of truth, in the midst of deficient,
redundant, or conflicting testimony. "The men
who wrote history," says Mr Dowling, speaking of
the times in question, "did not write by rule; they
only put down what they had seen, what they had
heard, what they knew. Very many of them did
what they did as a matter of moral duty. The
result was something *sui generis ;* it was not even
what *we* call history at all. It was, if I may so
speak, something more, an actual admeasurement
rather than a picture; or, if a picture, it was
painted in a style which had all the minute accuracy
and homely reality of the most domestic of the
Flemish masters, not the lofty hyperbole of the

Roman school, nor the obtrusive splendour, not less unnatural, of the Venetian. In a word, history, as a subject of criticism, is an art, a noble and beautiful *art ;* the historical writings of the Middle Ages is *nature.*"

Allusion is made in this passage to the peculiarity in monastic historiography, that it proceeded from the motive of religious obedience. This must always have been the case from the monastic profession; however, we have here, in addition to the presumption, actual evidence, and not on one occasion only, of the importance which the Benedictine Order attached to these notices and memorials of past times. In the year 1082, for instance, the Abbot Marquand of New Corbie in Saxony seems to have sent an order to all churches and monasteries subject to his rule, to send to him severally the chronicles of their own places. Abbot Wichbold repeated the order sixty years later, and Abbot Thierry in 1337 addressed to the provosts and rectors subject to him, a like injunction. Again, in 1481 the Abbot of Erfurdt addressed a letter to the Fathers of the Reform of Bursfeld, with the view of persuading them to enter into a similar undertaking. "If you were to agree among yourselves," he says, "and make a statute to the effect that every Prelate is under an obligation to compose annals and histories of his monastery, what could be better, what more useful, what more interesting, whether for knowing or for reading?"

It is easier to conjecture what those literary

works would be, in which a Benedictine would find
himself at liberty to engage, than to pretend to
point out those from which his vocation would debar
him; yet Mabillon, equally with De Rancé, implied
that all subjects do not come alike to him. Here
we are recalled to the well-known controversy
between these two celebrated men. The Abbot
of La Trappe, the Cistercian De Rancé, writing to
his own people, put forth some statements on the
subject of the studies proper to a monk, which
seemed to reflect upon the learned Maurists.
Mabillon, one of them, replied, in a learned vindication of himself and his brethren. The Abbot had
maintained that study of whatever kind should
be kept in strict subordination to manual labour,
and should not extend to any books except the
Scriptures and the ascetic treatises of the Fathers.
Mabillon, on the other hand, without denying the
necessity of manual labour, to which the Maurists
themselves devoted an hour a day, seemed to allow
to the Benedictine the free cultivation of the intellect, and an unlimited range of studies. When
they explained themselves, each combatant would
appear to have asserted more than he could successfully maintain; yet after all there was a considerable difference of view between them, which could
not be removed. The critical question was, whether
certain historical instances, which Mabillon urged
in his favour, were to be considered exceptions or
not to the rule of St Benedict. For ourselves, we
have certainly maintained in an earlier page of

this article, that such instances as Alcuin, Paschasius, or Lanfranc are no fair specimens of the
Benedictine profession, and must not be taken to
represent the monks generally. Lest, however, in
saying this, we may be thought to be evading the
testimony of history, as adduced by a writer,
authoritative at once by his learning and as
spokesman of the great Congregation of St Maur,
we think it well to extract in our behalf some of
his own admissions, which seem to us fully to bear
out what we were laying down above about the
spirit and mission of his Order.

For instance, he frankly concedes, or rather
maintains, that the scholastic method of teaching
theology and philosophy is foreign to the profession
of a Benedictine, as such. "Why," he asks,
"need we cultivate these sciences in the way of
disputation? Why not as positive sciences, explaining questions and resolving doubts, as they
occur? Why is it not more than enough for
religious pupils to be instructed in the more necessary principles of the science, and thereby to make
progress in the study of the Scriptures and the
Fathers? What need of this perpetual syllogising
in form, and sharp answers to innumerable objec-
tions, as is the custom in the schools?" Elsewhere
he contrasts the mode of teaching a subject, as
adopted by the early Fathers, with that which
the schoolmen introduced. " The reasonings of
the Fathers," he says, " are so full, so elegantly
set forth, as to be everywhere redolent of the

F

sweetness and vigour of Christian eloquence, whereas scholastic theology is absolutely dry and sterile." Elsewhere he says, that "in the study of Holy Scripture consists the entire science of monks." Again, he says of Moral Theology, "As monks are rarely destined to the cure of souls, it does not seem necessary that they should give much time to the science of Morals." And, though of course he does not forbid them the study of history, which we have seen to be so congenial to their calling, yet he observes of this study when pursued to its full extent, "It seems to cause much dissipation of mind, which is prejudicial to that inward compunction of heart, which is so especially fitted to the holy life of a monk." Again, observing that the examination of ancient MSS. was the special occupation of the Maurists in his time, he says, "They who give themselves to this study have the more merit with God, in that they have so little praise with men. Moreover, it obliges them to devote the more time to solitude, which ought to be their chief delight. I confess it is a most irksome and unpleasant labour; however, it gives much less trouble than transcription, which was the most useful work of our early monks." Elsewhere, speaking of the celebrated Maurist editions of the Fathers, he observes, "Labour, such as this, which is undergone in silence and in quietness, is especially compatible with true tranquillity of mind, and the mastery of the passions, provided we labour as a duty, and not for glory."

We trust the reader will be so good as to keep in mind that we are all along speaking of the Benedictine life *historically*, and as we might speak of any other historical *fact ;* not venturing at all on what would be the extreme presumption of any quasi-doctrinal or magisterial exposition of it, which belongs to those only who have actually imbibed its tradition. This being clearly understood, we think we may interpret Mabillon to mean that (be the range of studies lawful to a monk what it may) still, whatever literary work requires such continuous portions of time as not to admit of being suspended at a moment's notice, whatever is so interesting that other duties seem dull and heavy after it, whatever so exhausts the power of attention as to incapacitate for attention for other subjects, whatever makes the mind gravitate towards the creature, is inconsistent with monastic simplicity. Accordingly, we should expect to find that controversy was uncongenial to the Benedictine, because it excited the mind, and metaphysical investigations, because they fatigued it; and, when we met such instances as St Paschasius or St Anselm, we should deal with them as they came and as we could. Moreover, we should not look to a Benedictine for any elaborate and systematic work on the history of doctrine, or of heresy, or any course of patristical theology, or any extended ecclesiastical history, or any philosophical disquisitions upon history, as implying a grasp of innumerable details, and the

labour of using a mass of phenomena to the elucida-
tion of a theory, or of bringing a range of multi-
farious reading to bear upon one point; and that,
because such efforts of mind require either an
energetic memory devoted to matters of time and
place, or, instead of the tranquil and plodding
study of one book after another, the presence of a
large library, and the distraction of a vast number
of books handled all at once, not for perusal, but
for reference.   Perhaps we are open to the charge
of refining, in attempting to illustrate the principle
which we seem to ourselves to detect in the Benedictine tradition; but the principle itself which we
have before us is clear enough, and is expressed in
the advice which is given to us by a sacred writer:
" The words of the wise are as goads, and nails
deeply fastened in; *more than these, my son, require
not :* of making many books there is no end, and
much study is an affliction of the flesh."

To test the truth of this view of the Benedictine
mission, we cannot do better than appeal as a
palmary instance to the Congregation of St Maur,
an intellectual school of Benedictines assuredly.
Now what, in matter of fact, is the character of its
works? It has no Malebranche, no Thomassin, no
Morinus; it has no Bellarmine, no Suarez, no
Petavius; it has no Tillemont or Fleury,—all of
whom were more or less its contemporaries; but
it has a Montfaucon, it has a Mabillon, it has a
Sainte Marthe, a Coustant, a Sabbatier, a Martene,
—men of immense learning and research; it has

collators and publishers of MSS. and of inscriptions, editors of the text and of the versions of Holy Scripture, editors and biographers of the Fathers, antiquarians, annalists, paleographists,—with scholarship indeed, and criticism, and theological knowledge, admirable as often as elicited by the particular subject on which they are directly employed, but conspicuously subordinate to it.

If we turn to other contemporary Congregations of St Benedict we are met by the same phenomenon. Their labours have been of the same laborious, patient, tranquil kind. The first name which occurs to us is that of Augustine Calmet, of the Congregation of St Vanne. His works are biblical and antiquarian;—a literal Comment on Scripture with Dissertations, a dictionary of the Bible, a Comment on the Benedictine Rule, a history of Lorraine. We cast our eyes round the library, in which we happen at the moment to be writing; what Benedictine authors meet them? There is Ceillier, also of the Congregation of St Vanne; Bertholet, of the same Congregation; Cardinal Aguirre of Salamanca; Cressy of Douai; Pez of Mölk on the Danube; Lumper of St George in the Hercynian Forest; Brockie of the Scotch College at Ratisbon; Reiner of the English Congregation. Their works are of the same complexion,—historical antiquarian, biographical, patristical,—calling to mind the line of study traditionally pursued by a modern ecclesiastical congregation, the Italian Oratory. We do not speak of Ziegelbauer, François and other Benedictines who might be added, because they have confined themselves to Benedictine Antiquities, and every order will write about itself.

And so of the Benedictine Literature from first to last. Ziegelbauer, who has just been mentioned, has written four folio volumes on the subject, Now one of them is devoted to a catalogue and an account of Benedictine authors;—of these, those on Scripture and Positive Theology occupy 110 pages; those on history, 300; those on scholastic theology, 12; those on polemics, 12; those on moral theology, 6. This surprising contrast may be an exaggeration of the fact, because there is much of repetition and digression in his survey, and his biographical notices vary in length; but, after all allowances for such accidental unfairness in the list, the result must surely be considered as strikingly confirmatory of the account which we have been giving.

But we must cut short an investigation which, though imperfect for the illustration of its subject, is already long for the patience of the reader. All human works are exposed to vicissitude and decay; and that the great Order of which we have been writing should in the lapse of thirteen centuries have furnished no instances of that general law, is the less to be expected, in proportion to the extent of its territory, the independence of its separate houses, and the local varieties of its constitution. To say that peace may engender selfishness, and humility become a cloak for indolence, and a country life may be an epicurean luxury, is only to enunciate the over-true maxim, that every virtue has a vice for its first cousin. *Usum non tollit abusus ;* and the circumstance that Benedictine life admits of corruption into a mode of living which is not Benedictine, but its very contradictory, cannot surely be made an argument against its meritorious innocence, its resolute cheerfulness, and its strenuous tranquillity. We are told to be like little children; and where shall we find a more striking instance than is here afforded us of that union of simplicity and reverence, that clear perception of the unseen, yet recognition of the mysterious, which is the characteristic of the first years of human existence? To the monk heaven was next door; he formed no plans, he had no cares; the ravens of his father Benedict were ever at his side. He " went forth " in his youth " to his work and to his labour " until the evening of life; if he lived a day longer, he did a day's work more; whether he lived many days or few, he laboured on to the end of them. He had no wish to see further in advance of his journey, than where he was to make his next stage. He ploughed and sowed, he prayed, he meditated, he studied, he wrote, he taught, and then he died and went to heaven. He made his way into the labyrinthine forest, and he cleared just so much of space as his dwelling required, suffering the high solemn trees and the deep pathless thicket to close him in. And when he began to build, his architecture was suggested by the scene,—not the scientific and masterly conception of a great whole with many parts, as the Gothic style in a later age, but plain and inartificial, the adaptation of received fashions to his own purpose, and an addition of chapel to chapel, and a wayward growth of cloister, according to the occasion, with half-concealed shrines and unexpected recesses, with paintings on the wall as by a second thought, with an absence of display and a wild, irregular beauty, like that of the woods by which he was at first surrounded. And when he would employ his mind, he turned to Scripture, the book of books, and there he found a special response to the peculiarities of his vacation; for there supernatural truths stand forth as the trees and flowers of Eden in a divine disorder, as some awful intricate garden or paradise, which he enjoyed the more because he could not catalogue its wonders. Next he read the Holy Fathers, and there again he recognised a like ungrudging profusion and careless wealth of precept and consolation. And when he began to compose, still he did so after that mode which nature and revelation had taught him, avoiding curious knowledge, content with incidental ignorance, passing from subject to subject with little regard to system, or care to penetrate beyond his own homestead of thought,—and writing, not with the sharp logic of disputants, or the subtle analysis of philosophers, but with the one aim of reflecting in his pages, as in a faithful mirror, the words and works of the Almighty, as they confronted him, whether in Scripture and the Fathers, or in that " mighty maze " of deeds and events, which men call the world's history, but which to him was a Providential Dispensation.

Here the beautiful character in life and death of St Bede naturally occurs to us, who is, in his person and his writings, as truly the pattern of a Benedictine, as is St Thomas of a Dominican; and with an extract from the letter of Cuthbert to Cuthwin concerning his last hours, which, familiarly as it is known, is always pleasant to read, we break off our subject for the present.

" He was exceedingly oppressed," says Cuthbert of St Bede, " with shortness of breathing, though without pain, before Easter Day, for about a fortnight; but he rallied, and was full of joy and gladness, and gave thanks to Almighty God day and night and every hour, up to Ascension Day; and he gave us, his scholars, daily lectures, and passed the rest of the day in singing the Psalms, and the night too in joy and thanksgiving, except the scanty time which he gave to sleep. And as soon as he woke, he was busy in his customary way, and he never ceased with uplifted hands giving thanks to God. I solemnly protest, never have I seen or heard of anyone who was so diligent in thanksgiving.

" He sang that sentence of the blessed Apostle Paul, ' It is a dreadful thing to fall into the hands of the Living God,' and many other passages of Scripture, in which he warned us to shake off the slumber of the soul, by anticipating our last hour.

And he sang some verses of his own in English also,
to the effect that no one could be too well prepared
for his end—viz., in calling to mind, before he
departs hence, what good or evil he has done, and
how his judgment will lie. And he sang too the
antiphons, of which one is, ' O King of Glory, Lord
of Angels, who this day hast ascended in triumph
above all the heavens, leave us not orphans, but
send the promise of the Father upon us, the Spirit
of Truth, alleluia.' And when he came to the
words, ' leave us not orphans,' he burst into tears,
and wept much. He said, too, ' God scourgeth
every son whom he receiveth,' and, with St Ambrose, ' I have not so lived as to be ashamed to
have been among you, nor do I fear to die, for we
have a good Lord.'

" In those days, besides our lectures and the
Psalmody, he was engaged in two works; he was
translating into English the Gospel of St John as
far as the words, ' But what are these among so
many,' and some extracts from the *Notæ* * of
Isidore. On the Tuesday before Ascension Day,
he began to suffer still more in his breathing, and
his feet were slightly swollen. However, he went
through the day, dictating cheerfully, and he kept
saying from time to time, ' Take down what I say
quickly, for I know not how long I am to last, or
whether my Maker will not take me soon.' He

---

* The Bollandists have not been able to determine which
of St Isidore's works is here intended ; it is not wonderful
that we have as little succeeded in the attempt.

seemed to us to be quite aware of the time of his
going, and he passed that night in giving of thanks,
without sleeping. As soon as morning broke,
that is on the Wednesday, he urged us to make
haste with the writing which we had begun. We
did so till nine o'clock, when we walked in procession with the Relics of the Saints, according to
the usage of that day. But one of our party said
to him, 'Dearest Master, one chapter is still wanting; can you bear our asking you about it?' He
answered, 'I can bear it; take your pen and be
ready, and write quickly.' At three o'clock he
said to me, 'Run fast, and call our priests, that I
may divide among them some little gifts which I
have in my box.' When I had done this in much
agitation, he spoke to each, urging and intreating
them all to make a point of saying Masses and
prayers for him. Thus he passed the day in joy
until the evening, when the above-named youth
said to him, 'Dear Master, there is yet one sentence
not written;' he answered, 'Write quickly.'
Presently the youth said, 'Now it is written;' he
replied, 'Good, thou hast said the truth; *con-
summatum est;* take my head into thy hands, for
it is very pleasant to me to sit facing my old praying
place, and thus to call upon my Father.' And so, on
the floor of his cell, he sang, 'Glory be to Father,
Son, and Holy Ghost,' and, just as he had said
'Holy Ghost,' he breathed his last, and went to the
realms above."

It is remarkable that this flower of the Bene-

dictine school died on the same day as St Philip
Neri,—Thursday, May 26th, which in Bede's
instance was Ascension Day, and in Philip's the
feast of Corpus Christi. It was fitting that two
saints should go to heaven together, whose mode of
going thither was the same; both of them singing,
praying, working, and guiding others in joy and
exultation, till their very last hour.

The
Benedictine   Centuries

WE read in history of great commanders, who,
when an overwhelming force was directed against
them on the plain, and success was for the time
impossible, submitted to necessity, and, with plans
afterwards to be developed, retired up the mountain
passes in their rear, where nature had provided a
safe halting-place for brave men who could not
advance, and would not turn in flight.   There,
behind the lofty crag, the difficult morass, and the
thick wood, they nursed their confidence of victory,
and waited patiently for an issue, which was not
less certain because it was delayed.   On came the
haughty foe with cries of defiance; and, when at
length he thought he had them at his mercy, he
found that first he must do battle with the adaman-
tine rocks, which sternly rose up in defence of
fugitives who had invoked their aid.   Then he
stood for a while irresolute, till the difficulties of
his position ended his deliberation and forced upon
him a retreat in his turn, while the lately besieged

hosts were once more in motion, and pressed upon the baffled foe, who had neither plan of campaign nor base of operations to fall back upon.

Such is the history of Christian civilisation. It gave way before the barbarians of the north and the fanatics of the south; it fled into the wilderness with its own books and those of the old social system which it was succeeding. It obeyed the direction given it in the beginning,—when persecuted in one place, to flee away to another; but at length the hour of retribution came, and it advanced into the territories from which it had retired. St Benedict is the historical emblem of its retreat, and St Dominic of its return.

We do not say that its retreat in the first centuries was in order to its return in the mediæval. There was no oracular voice which proclaimed what would be the course of the war; no secret tradition which whispered to the initiated the tactic that ought to be pursued. It is a sufficient explanation of the double movement, that they who feel their weakness are used to give way, and they who feel their strength are used to push forward. The corruptions of Roman society caused Christians to despair of ever mending it, and to look out for that better world which was destined to supersede it. The evil which they experienced, the good for which they sighed, the promise in which they confided, wrought in them the persuasion that the end of all things was at hand; and this persuasion made them patient under inconveniences which were only temporary. "Behold, my brethren," says Pope Gregory about the year 600, "we already see with our eyes, what we are used to hear in prophecy. Day by day is the world assaulted by fresh and thickening blows. Out of that innumerable Roman *plebs* what a remnant are ye at this day! yet incessant scourges are still in action; sudden adversities thwart you; new and unforeseen slaughters wear you away. For, as in youth the body is in vigour, the chest is strong, the neck muscular, and the arms plump, but in old age the stature is bent, the neck is withered and stooping, the chest pants, the energies are feeble, and breath is wanting for the words; so the world too once was vigorous, robust for the increase of its kind, green in its health, and opulent in its resources, but now on the contrary it is laden with the weight of years, and is fast sinking into the grave by its ever-multiplying maladies. Beware then of giving your heart to that, which, as even your senses tell you, cannot last for ever." Commonly the presentiment wore a more definitely supernatural expression than is found in this extract. Not sense merely, but the prophecies were invoked, which spoke of that great enemy of the Church, who was to be the herald of the second Advent; and the rudiments of a new order of things were descried in the manifest tokens of an expiring world.

In all times indeed the multitude, whether from religious feeling or from superstition, is prone to portend some impending catastrophe from the occurrence of any startling phenomenon of nature. An eclipse, a comet, a volcanic eruption, is to them the omen of coming evil.   But in the early centuries of the Church, the expectation extended to the learned and the saintly.   It was the posture of mind of professors and doctors.   As St Gregory looked out for Antichrist in the sixth century, so did the Martyrs of Lyons in the second, St Cyprian in the third, St Hilary and St Chrysostom in the fourth, and St Jerome in the fifth.   It was the sober judgment of the wisest and most charitable, that the world was too bad to mend, and that destruction was close upon it.

What would be the practical result of such a belief?   That which we have partly described in an article, of which the present is a continuaton ;* evidently, to leave the world to itself.   Evils which threaten to continue, we try to remedy; but what was the use of spending one's strength in reforming a state of things, which would go to pieces, if let alone, and, if ever so much meddled with, would go to pieces too, nay, the sooner perhaps, for the meddling?   It was then that the prevalent disposition, as we have said, of Christians of the first centuries, and no irrational disposition, either to leave the world, or to put up with it, not to set about influencing it.   "Let us go hence," said the angels in the doomed sanctuary of the

* We may here set right our translation of the word "siligo" in that article.   It is rye, as well as wheat, and has that meaning in the passage quoted.

chosen people. "Come ye out of her, my people," was the present bidding of inspiration. Those who would be perfect, obeyed it, and became monks. Monachism therefore was a sort of recognised emigration from the old world. St Antony had found out a new coast, the true *eldorado* or gold country; and on the news of it thousands took their departure year after year for the diggings in the desert. The monks of Egypt alone soon became an innumerable host. As times got worse, Basil in the East, and Benedict in the West, put themselves at the head of fresh colonies, bound for the land of perpetual peace. There they sat them down, over against Babylon, and waited for the coming judgment and the end of all things. Those who remained in the world, waited too. To undergo patiently what was, to make the best of it, to use it, as far as it could be used, for religious purposes, was their wisdom and their resolve. If they took another course, they would be wasting strength and hope upon a shadow, and losing the present for a future which would never come. They had no large designs or profound policy. It was their aim that things should just last their time. They patched them up as best they might; they made shift, and lived from hand to mouth; and they followed events, rather than created them. Nor, when they undertook great labours, and began works pregnant with consequences, did they perceive whither they were going.

How different in this respect is the spirit of the

G

first Gregory, already cited, from that of Hildebrand the Seventh! Gregory the First did not understand his own act, when he converted the Anglo-Saxons; nor Ambrose, when he put Theodosius to penance. The great Christian Fathers laid anew the foundations of the world, while they thought that its walls were tottering to the fall, and that they already saw the fires of judgment through the chinks. They refuted Arianism, which they named the forerunner of the last woe, with reasonings which were to live for ages; and they denounced the preachers of a carnal millennium, without anticipating that glorious temporal reign of the saints which was to be fulfilled in mediæval times. They propounded broad principles, but did not carry them out into their inevitable consequences. How slow were they to define doctrine, when disputes arose about its meaning or its bearing! How little jealous were they of imperial encroachments on ecclesiastical rights, when they are viewed by the side of the great Popes who came after them! How tamely do they conduct themselves, when the civil magistrate interferes with their jurisdiction, or takes the initiative in points of discipline or order, in questions of property, and matrimonial causes! How contented or resigned are they to avail themselves of such education as the state provided for their use; sending their children to the pagan schools, before they have teachers of their own, and, even when at length they have them, adopting the *curriculum* of studies which those pagan schools had devised!

In fact, " the wish was father to the thought."
Religious minds will always desire, will always be
prone to believe, the approach of that happier order
of things which sooner or later is to be.   This hope
was the form in which the deep devotion of those
primitive times showed itself; and if it did not
continue in its full expression beyond them, this
was because experience had thrown a new light
upon the course of Divine Providence.   With the
multitude, indeed, as we have said, who know little
of history, and in whom religious fear is a chief
element, the anticipation of the last day revived,
and revives, from time to time.   At the end of the
tenth century, when a thousand years had passed
over the Church, the sense of impending destruction
was so vivid as even to affect the transfer and
disposal of property, and the repair of sacred
buildings.   However, when we seek in theologians
for the apprehension, we shall find that it is a
characteristic of the old Empire far more than of
the barbarian kingdoms which succeeded to it.
The barbarian world was young, as the Roman
world was effete.   Youth is the season of hope;
and, according as things looked more cheerful, so
did they look more lasting, and to-day's sunshine
became the sufficient promise of a long summer.
A fervent preacher here or there, St Norbert or
St Vincent Ferrer, may have had forebodings of
the end of all things; or an astrologer or a schis-
matising teacher may have traded on the
belief; but the men of gravity and learning after

the time of Gregory, for the most part, set their faces against speculations about the future.

Bede, after speaking of the six ages of the world, says, that " as no one of the former ages has consisted exactly of a thousand years, it follows that the sixth too, under which we live, is of uncertain length, known to him alone who has bidden his servants watch. For," he continues, " whereas all saints naturally love the hour of his advent, and desire it to be near, still, we run into danger, if we presume to conclude or to proclaim, either that the hour is near or that it is far off." Raban and Adson, who witnessed or heard of the splendours of Charlemagne, go so far as to indulge the vision of a great king of the Franks, who, in time to come, is to reign religiously, ere the fulfilment of the bad times of the end. Theodulf indeed predicts that they were coming; but, even when the popular excitement was at its height, in the last years of the tenth century, Richard and Abbo of Fleury, and the Adson above mentioned, set themselves against it. Hardly was the dreaded crisis over, when men took heart, and began to restore and decorate the churches; hardly had the new century run its course, when Pope Paschal the Second held a Council at Florence against the archbishop of that city, who had preached of the coming end. Such was the change of sentiment which followed after the Pontificate of St Gregory, the last and saddest of a line of Fathers who thought the world was on the verge of dissolution.

The names which we have been introducing, show that, among these converts from a despairing view of things, were Benedictine monks, members of those very associations which had given up the world as lost, and had quitted it accordingly. And their position in their own body is sufficient evidence that what they held, their brethren held too; and that the actual changes in the social fabric had been followed by a change of sentiment also in these religious bodies. When we look into history, to see what these authors were, as well as who, we find the fact plain beyond all denial; for the monk Alcuin was Charlemagne's instructor, and head of the school of the palace; the monk Theodulf was a political *employé* of the same Emperor, and Bishop of Orleans; and the monk Raban was Archbishop of Mayence. How could the cloister-loving monk have come to such places of station, without some singular change in his sentiments? And these instances, it must be allowed, are only samples of a phenomenon which is not uncommon in these centuries. Here then we have something to explain. Why should Benedictines leave those sweet country-homes which St Benedict bequeathed to them, for the haunts of men, the seats of learning, archiepiscopal sees, and kings' courts? St Jerome had said, when Monachism was young: "If the priest's office be your choice, if a bishop's work or dignity be your attraction, live a town life, and save your soul in saving others. But, if you wish to be a monk, that is a solitary, in fact as well as in name, what have you to do with towns?" "A monk's office," he says elsewhere, "is not a teacher's but a mourner's, who bewails either himself or the world. This, doubtless, was the primary aim and badge of the religious institute; and if, among uncongenial offices, there be one more uncongenial to it than another, it was that of a ruler or a master. The monk did not lecture, teach, controvert, lay down the law, or give the word of command; and for this simple reason, because he did not speak at all, because he was bound to silence. He had given up the use of his tongue, and could neither be preacher nor disputant. It follows, we repeat, that a singular change must have taken place by the ninth century in the ecclesiastical position of a monk, when we find instances of his acting so differently from St Jerome's teaching and example in the fifth.

We touched, in our former article, upon this seeming anomaly in the history of the Benedictines, while we were describing them in outline; if we did not then dwell upon it and investigate its limits, this was because we thought it advisable first to trace out the general idea of the monastic state, with as little interruption as was possible, without risking the confusion which would arise in our delineation from a premature introduction of the historical modifications to which that idea has actually been subjected. Now, however, the time has come for taking up what in that former sketch we passed over; and we propose in this article accordingly, after a brief reference to the circumstances under which these modifications appeared, and to the extent to which they spread, to direct attention to the principal instance of them—viz., the literary employments of the monks, and to show how singularly, after all, these employments, as carried out, were in keeping with the main idea of the monastic rule, even though they seem at first sight scarcely contained in its letter. We stated, when we originally opened our subject, that the substance of the monastic life was "summa quies"; that its object was rest, its state retirement, and its occupations such as were unexacting, and had their end in themselves. That the literature in question was consistent with these conditions will be clearly seen, when we come to describe it; first, however, let us allude to the circumstances which called for it, and the hold which it had upon the general body.

It is rare, indeed, to find the profession and the history of any institution running exactly in one and the same groove. The political revolutions which issued in the rule of Charlemagne, changing, as they did, the currents of the world, and the pilotage of St Peter's bark, became a severe trial of the consistency of an Order like the Benedictine, of which the maxims and the aims are grave, definite, and fixed. Demands of action and work would be made on it by the exigencies of the times, at variance with its genius, and it would find itself in the dilemma of failing in efficiency on the one hand, or in faithfulness to its engagements on the other. It would be incurring either the impatience of society, which it disappointed, or the remonstrances of its own subjects, whom it might be considered to betray.

And indeed a greater shock can hardly be fancied than that which would overtake the peaceful inhabitant of the cloister, on his finding that, after all, he so intimately depended still upon the world, which he had renounced, and that the changes which were taking place in its condition, were affecting his own. Such men, whether senators like Paulinus or courtiers like Arsenius, or legionaries like Martin, had one and all in their respective places and times left the responsibilities of earth for the anticipations of heaven. They had sought, in the lonely wood or the silent mountain top, the fair uncorrupted form of nature, which spoke only of the Creator. They had retired into deserts, where they could have no enemies but such as fast and prayer could subdue. They had gone where the face of man was not, except as seen in pale, ascetic apparitions like themselves. They had secured some refuge, whence they might look round at the sick world in the distance, and see it die. But, when that last hour came, it did but frustrate all their hopes, and, for an old world at a distance, they found they had a young world close to them. The old order of things died indeed, but a new order took its place, and they themselves, by no

will or expectation of their own, were in no small
measure its very life.   The lonely Benedictine rose
from his knees, and found himself a city.   This was
the case, not merely here or there, but everywhere ;
Europe was new mapped, and the monks were the
principle of mapping.   They had grown into large
communities, into abbeys, into corporations with
civil privileges, into landholders with tenants, serfs,
and baronial neighbours; they had become centres
of population, the schools of the most cherished
truths, the shrines of the most sacred confidences.
They found themselves priests, rulers, legislators,
feudal lords, royal counsellors, missionary preachers,
controversialists;   and they comprehended that,
unless they fled anew from the face of man, as St
Antony in the beginning, they must bid farewell
to the hope of leading St Antony's life.

In this choice of difficulties, when there was a
duty to stay and a duty to take flight, the monastic
bodies were not unwilling to come to a compromise
with the age, and, reserving their fidelity to St
Benedict, to undertake those functions to which
both the world and the Church called them.   Such,
that is, for the most part, was the resolve of those
who found themselves in this perplexity;   but it
could not be supposed that there were no Antonies
on earth still, and that these would be satisfied to
adopt it.   On the contrary, there were holy men
who were but impelled into a reaction of the most
rigid asceticism by the semblance of a reconcilia-
tion between their brethren and the world.   Such

was St Romuald in the tenth century, the founder
of the Camaldolese, who, through a long life of in-
credible austerities, was ever forming new monastic
stations, and leaving them, when formed, from love
of solitude. Such St Bruno, the founder of the
Carthusians, whose conversion, as described in the
well-known legend, points to the union in his day
of intellectual gifts and dissoluteness of life.
" Come, dear friends," he is represented as saying
to some companions, " what is to become of us?
If a man of this doctor's rank and repute, of such
literary, such scientific attainments, of such
seeming-virtuous life, of so wide a reputation, is
thus indubitably damned, what is to become of
poor creatures of no estimation, such as we are? "
Such, again, was St Stephen of Grandimont, who,
when two Cardinals came to see and wonder at
him in his French desert, excused himself by saying,
" How could we serve churches and undertake
cures, who are dead to the world, and have every
member of our body cut off from this life, with
neither feet to walk, nor tongues to speak withal?"
These, and others such, sought out for themselves
a seclusion and silence most congenial to the
original idea of monachism, but incompatible with
those active duties,—missions, the pastoral office,
teaching in the schools, and disputations with
heresy,—which at the time there were none but
monks to fulfil.

Would that nothing worse than the demand of
such sarced duties brought the monasteries into

the world, and drove these reformers into the
desert! It cannot be denied that the gravest
moral disorders had arisen within their walls; and
that, partly indeed from the seductions of ease,
wealth, and the homage of mankind, but in a great
measure also from the political troubles of the times,
which exposed them to the tyranny of the military
chief, or the violence of the marauder. Relaxation
will easily take place in a religious community,
when, from whatever circumstance, it cannot
observe its rule; and what orderly observance
could there be, when the country round about was
the seat of war and rapine? Nay, a simpler process of monastic degeneracy followed from the
high hand of military power. Kings seized the
temporalities of the abbeys for their favourites,
and made licentious soldiers bishops and abbots;
and these, by their terrors and their bribes, fostered
a lax irreligious party in the heart of these communities up and down the country. This part of
the history, however, does not concern us in these
pages, which are devoted to the consideration of
the real work of the Benedictine, not to the injuries
or interruptions which it has sustained, or to
corruptions which are not its own.

On the other hand, not kings alone interfered
with St Benedict. A not less forcible overruling of
his tradition took place from another quarter,
where there was authority for the act, and where
nothing would be done except on religious principles and with religious purposes. It was a more

serious interference, for the very reason that it was a legal one, proceeding from the Church herself. According to the maxim, " sacramenta propter homines," she has never hesitated to consider, in this sense of the maxim, that " the end justifies the means; " and since Regulars of whatever sort are her own creation, she can of course alter, or adapt, or change, or bring to nought, according as her needs require, the institutions which she has created. Necessity has no law, and charity has no reserves; and she has acted accordingly. She brought the Benedictine from his cloister into the political world; but, as far as she did so, let it be observed, it was her act, and not his. If, then, on account of the necessities of the day, she has over-ruled his resolve, and made him do what neither his tradition nor his wishes suggested, such instances cannot fairly be taken, either as specimens of Benedictine work, or as modifications of the Benedictine idea.

And such cases abound. St Benedict himself had with difficulty contemplated the idea of a priest in the ranks of his children; laying it down in his Rule, " If a priest asks to be received in any monastery, his request must not quickly be granted; but if he persists, the whole discipline of the rule is binding on him without any relaxation " (c. 60). But Pope Gregory, who had himself been torn violently from the cloister, spared his religious brethren as little as he had himself been spared. He made a number of them bishops. From his

own convent on the Cælian he sent Augustine and
his companions to be apostolic missionaries to the
Anglo-Saxons, and he designed to put the entire
episcopate and priesthood of the newly converted
race, and thereby their secular concerns, into the
hands of the monks. As to the Archbishops of
Canterbury, they actually were monks down to the
twelfth century. This is but a specimen of what
was carried out by the Holy See on the Continent
in the centuries which followed Gregory; but here
too the Pope's action is external to the Benedictines,
who are as little compromised by his consecrating
hand as by the iron glove of the feudal tyrant.

To whatever extent, however, these innovations
went, whether they were simple profanations, or
were made and ratified by the wise policy of those
who had a right to make them, and whatever show
they make in history from the circumstance of their
necessary connection with public events, with
principal cities, and with prominent men, we
cannot speak of them as constituting any great
exception to the monastic discipline, or as exerting
any considerable influence on the monastic spirit,
till we have surveyed the religious institutions of
Christendom as a whole, and measured them by
the side of the general view thus obtained. We
had occasion in our former article to allude to the
condition of the early monks, their various families,
the rise of the Benedictines, and the process of
assimilation and absorption, by which at length St
Benedict gathered under his own rule the disciples

of St Martin, St Cæsarius, and St Columban. And
even when the whole monastic body was Benedictine, it was not on that account moulded upon
one type, or depended upon one centre. As it
had not spread out from one origin, so it neither
was homogeneous in its construction, nor simple
and concordant in its action. It propagated itself
variously, and had much of local character in its
secondary dispositions. We cannot be certain
what it was in one place, by knowing what it was
in another. One house attained more nearly to
what may be called its normal idea than another,
and therefore we have no right to argue that such
quasi-secularisations as we have noticed, extended
much further than those particular cases which
history has handed down to us.

And then, on the other hand, we must bear in
mind how vast was the whole multitude of persons
who professed the monastic life, and, compared
with it, how small was the number of those who
were called away to active political duties or who
gave themselves to study. They might all be
subtracted from the sum-total of religious, and, as
far as number goes, they would not have been missed.
We have already referred to the exuberance of
Egyptian monachism. Antony left to Pachomius
the rule of 50,000. Posthumus of Memphis pre-
sided over 5000; Ammon over 3000. In the one
city of Oxyrinchus there were 10,000. Hilarion in
Syria had from 2000 to 3000. Martin of Gaul was
followed to the grave by 2000 of his disciples. At

that date, the sees of the whole of Christendom, according to Bingham, did not go much beyond 1700. If every bishop then had been a monk, the general character of monastic life would not have been much affected. In a later age, the monastery of Bangor contained 2000; that of Banchor, county Down, according to St Bernard, " many thousand monks," one of whom founded as many as 100 monasteries in various places. Again, the Episcopal Sees of France are given in the *Gallia Christiana* as 160, including the provinces of Utrecht, Cologne, and Treves; and precisely that number of monastic houses is said to have been founded in that country by St Maur alone, in the very first years of the Benedictines. Trithemius at the end of the fifteenth century numbers the Benedictine convents as 15,000; and, though we are not to suppose that each of them had the 2000 subjects which we find at Bangor, the lowest average will swell the sum-total of monks to a vast multitude. In the beginning of the previous century, a census of the Benedictines was taken by John the Twenty-second, to which Helyot refers, according to which the Order, from its commencement up to that time, had had 22,000 archbishops and bishops, and of saints alone 40,000. Vague calculations or statements are sufficient to represent general truths; it is difficult to determine what is the percentage of heroic virtue in a population of regulars; if we say at random, as many as five in the hundred, even at this high rate the Episcopal portion would be only a thirty-seventh part of the whole number of Benedictines.

More data, then, than we need, will be left to us in history to ascertain the monastic vocation, even though we strike out from the list of its disciples every monk who took any secular office, as of prelate, lecturer, or disputant; nay, though we formed all those who undertook such duties into evidence of an opposite mode of life.   But in fact, these very men, who in one way or another were engaged in work, which St Benedict has not recognised by name, are themselves specimens of fidelity to their founder, and impress the Benedictine type of sanctity upon their literary or political undertakings.   The proverb, "naturam expellas furca," etc., holds true of religion.   Whatever has life has in it a conservative principle, and a power of assimilation.   Where the religious spirit was strong, it would overcome obstacles in its exercise, and revive after overthrows, and would make for itself preternatural channels for its operations, when its legitimate course was denied to it. Neither the functions of an apostle, nor of a schoolmaster, are much akin to those of a monk; nevertheless, in a given individual, they may be reconciled, or the one merged in the other.   The Benedictine missionary soon relapsed into the laborious husbandman; the champion of the faith flung his adversary, and went back to his plough or his pen; the bishop, like Peter Damian, effected, or like Boniface, contemplated, a return in his old age to the cloister which he had left. As to the Schools of learning, it will be our business now to show how undisputatious was the master, and how unexciting the studies.

The rise and extension of these Schools seems to us as great an event in the history of the Order as the introduction of the sacerdotal office into the number of its functions. If Pope Gregory took a memorable step in turning monks of his convent into missionary bishops charged with the conversion of England, much more remarkable was the act of Pope Vitalian, in sending the old Greek monk Theodore to the same island, to fill the vacant see of Canterbury. We call it more remarkable, because it introduced an actual tradition into the Benedictine houses, and consecrated a system by authority. It is true that from an early date in the history of monachism, extensive learning had been combined with the profession of a monk. St Jerome was only too fond of the Cicero and Horace, whom he put aside; and, if out of the whole catalogue of ecclesiastics we had to select a literary Father, the monk Jerome, *par excellence*, would be he. In the next century Claudian Mamercus, of Vienne, employed the leisure which his monastic profession gave him to gain an extensive knowledge of Greek and Latin literature. He collected a library of Greek, Roman, and Christian books, " quam totam, monachus," says Sidonius of him, " virente in ævo, secreta bibit institutione." And in the century after, Cassiodorus, the contemporary

H

of St Benedict, is well known for combining sacred
and classical studies in his monastery. The
tradition, however, of the cloister was up to that
time against profane literature, and Theodore
reversed it.

This celebrated man made his appearance at the
end of the century which the missionary Augustine
opened, and just about the time when the whole
extent of England had been converted to the
Christian faith. He brought with him Greek as
well as Latin Classics, and set up schools for both
the learned languages in various parts of the
country. Henceforth the curriculum of the Seven
Sciences is found in the Benedictine schools.
From Theodore proceeded Egbert and the school
of York; from Egbert came Bede and the school of
Jarrow; from Bede, Alcuin, and the schools of
Charlemagne at Paris, Tours, and Lyons. From
these came Raban and the school of Fulda; from
Raban, Walafrid and the school of Richenau;
Lupus and the school of Ferrières. From Lupus,
Heiric, Remi, and the school of Rheims; from
Remi, Odo of Cluni; from the dependencies of
Cluni, the celebrated Gerbert, afterwards Pope
Sylvester the Second, and Abbo of Fleury, whom
we have already introduced to the reader's notice,
though not by name, in the former part of this
sketch, as repaying a portion of the debt which the
Franks owed to the Anglo-Saxons, by opening the
schools of Ramsey Abbey, after the inroad of the
Danes.

And now, at length, in addressing ourselves to the question, how such studies can be considered in keeping with the original idea of the monastic state, we think it right to repeat an explanation, which we made at an earlier stage of our discussion, to the effect that we are proposing nothing more than a survey of the venerable order of St Benedict from without; and we claim leave to do as much as this by the same right by which the humblest amongst us may freely and without offence gaze on sun, moon, and stars, and form his own private opinion, true or false, of their materials and their motions. And with this proviso, we remind the reader, if we have not sufficiently done so in our present pages, that the one object, immediate as well as ultimate, of Benedictine life, as history presents it to us, was to live in purity and to die in peace. The monk proposed to himself no great or systematic work, beyond that of saving his soul. What he did more than this, was the accident of the hour, spontaneous acts of piety, the sparks of mercy or beneficence, struck off in the heat, as it were, of his solemn religious toil, and done over almost as soon as they began to be. If to-day he cut down a tree, or relieved the famishing, or visited the sick, or taught the ignorant, or transcribed a page of Scripture, this was a good in itself, though nothing was added to it to-morrow. He cared little for knowledge, even theological, or for success, even though it was religious. It is the character of such a man to be contented, resigned,

patient, and incurious; to create or originate
nothing; to live by tradition. He does not analyse,
he marvels; his intellect attempts no comprehen-
sion of this multiform world, but on the contrary
it is hemmed in, and shut up within it. It recognises but one cause in nature and in human affairs,
and that is the First and Supreme; and why things
happen day by day in this way, and not in that, it
refers immediately to his will. It loves the
country, because it is his work; but " man made
the town," and he and his works are evil. This is
what may be called the Benedictine idea, then
viewed in the abstract; and, as being such, we gave
it the title of " poetical," when contrasted with that
of other religious orders; and we did so, because
we considered we saw in it a congeniality, *mutatis
mutandis*, to the spirit of a Poet, who has perhaps
greater title to that high name than anyone else,
as having received a wider homage, and that among
nations in time, place, and character, further
removed from each other.

Now supposing the historical portrait of the
Benedictine to be such as this, and that we were
further told that he was concerned with study and
with teaching, and then were asked, keeping in
mind the notion of his poetry of character, to guess
what books he studied and what sort of pupils he
taught, we should without much difficulty conclude
that Scripture would be his literature, and children
would be the members of his school. And if we were
further asked, what was likely to be the subject-

matter of the schooling imparted to these boys, probably we should not be able to make any guess at all; but we surely should not be very much surprised to be told, that the same spirit which led him to prefer the old basilicas for worship instead of any new architecture of his own inventing, and to honour his emperor or king with spontaneous loyalty more than by theological definitions, would also induce him, in the matter of education, to take up with the old books and subjects which he found ready to his hand in the pagan schools, as far as he could religiously do so, rather than venture on any experiments or system of his own. This, as we have already intimated, was the case. He adopted the Roman curriculum, professed the Seven Sciences, began with Grammar, that is, the Latin classics, and if he sometimes finished with them, it was because his boys left him ere he had time to teach them more. His choice of subjects was his fit recompense for choosing. He adopted the Latin writers from his love of prescription, because he found them in possession. But there were in fact no writings, after Scripture, more congenial, from their fresh and natural beauty, and their absence of intellectualism, to the monastic temperament. Such were his school-books; and, as "the boy is father of the man," the little monks, who heard them read or pored over them, when they grew up, filled the atmosphere of the monastery with the tasks and studies with which they had been imbued in their childhood.

For so it was, strange as it seems to our ideas, these boys were monks—monks as truly as those of riper years. About St Benedict's time the Latin Church innovated upon the discipline of former centuries, and allowed parents, not only to dedicate their infants to a religious life, but to do so without any power on the part of those infants, when they came to years of reason, to annul the dedication. This discipline continued for five or six centuries, beginning with the stern Spaniards, nor ending till shortly before the pontificate of Innocent the Third. Divines argued in behalf of it from the case of infant baptism, in which the sleeping soul, without being asked, is committed to the most solemn of engagements; from that of Isaac on the Mount, and of Samuel, and from the sanction of the Mosaic Law; and they would be confirmed in their course by the instances of compulsion, not uncommon in the early centuries, when high magistrates or wealthy heads of families were suddenly seized on by the populace or by synods, and against their remonstrances, tonsured, ordained, and consecrated, before they could well take breath and realise to themselves their change of station. Nor must we forget the old Roman law, the spirit of which they had inherited, and which gave to the father the power even of life and death over his refractory offspring.

However, childhood is not the age at which the severity of the law would be felt, which bound a man by his parent's acts to the service of the cloister. While these oblates were but children, they were pretty much like other children; they threw a grace over the stern features of monastic asceticism, and peopled the silent haunts of penance with a crown of bright innocent faces. "Silence was pleased," to use the poet's language, when it was broken by the cheerful, and sometimes, it must be confessed, unruly voices of a set of school-boys. These would sometimes, certainly, be inconveniently loud, especially as St Benedict did not exclude from his care lay-boys, destined for the world. It was more than the devotion of some good monks could bear; and they preferred some strict Reform, which, among its new provisions, prohibited the presence of these uncongenial associates. But, after all, it was no great evil to place before the eyes of austere manhood and unlovely age a sight so calculated to soften and to cheer. It was not adolescence, with its curiosity, its pride of knowledge, and its sensitiveness, with its disputes and emulations, with its exciting prizes and its impetuous breathless efforts, which St Benedict undertook to teach: he was no professor in a university. His convent was an infant school, a grammar school, and a seminary: it was not an academy. Indeed, the higher education in that day scarcely can be said to exist. It was a day of bloodshed and of revolution; before the time of life came, when the university succeeds the school, the student had to choose his profession. He became a clerk or a monk, or he became a soldier.

The fierce northern warriors, who had won for themselves the lands of Christendom with their red hands, rejoiced to commit their innocent offspring to the custody of religion and of peace. Nay, sometimes with the despotic will, of which we have just now spoken, they dedicated them, from or before their birth, to the service of Heaven. They determined that some at least of their lawless race should be rescued from the contamination of blood and licence, and should be set apart in sacred places to pray for their kindred. The little beings, of three or four or five years old, were brought in the arms of those who gave them life, to accept at their bidding the course in which that life was to run. They were brought into the sanctuary, spoke by the mouth of their parents, as at the font, put out their tiny hand for the sacred corporal to be wrapped round it, received the cowl and took their place as monks in the monastic community. In the first ages of the Benedictine Order, these children were placed on a level with their oldest brethren. They took precedence according to their date of admission, and the grey head gave way to them in choir and refectory, in junior to them in monastic standing. They even voted in the election of abbot, being considered to speak by divine instinct, as the child who cried out, " Ambrose is Bishop." If they showed waywardness in community meetings, inattention at choir, ill behaviour at table, which certainly was not an impossible occurrence, they were corrected by the nods, the words, or the blows of the grave brother who happened to be next them: it was not till an after time that they had a prefect of their own, except in school hours.

That harm came from this remarkable discipline is only the suggestion of our modern habits and ideas; that it was not expedient for all times follows from the fact that at a certain date it ceased to be permitted. However, that, in those centuries in which it was in force, its result was good, is seen in the history of those heroic men whom it nurtured, and might have been anticipated from the principle which it embodied. The monastery was intended to be the paternal home, not the mere refuge of the monk: it was an orphanage, not a reformatory; father and mother had abandoned him, and he grew up from infancy in the new family which had adopted him. He was a child of the house; there were stored up all the associations of his wondering boyhood, and there would lie the hopes and interests of his maturer years. He was to seek for sympathy in his brethren, and to give them his own in return. He lived and died in their presence. They prayed for his soul, cherished his memory, were proud of his name, and treasured his works. A pleasing illustration of this brotherly affection meets us in the life of Walafrid Strabo, Abbot of Richenau, whose poems, written by him when a boy of fifteen and eighteen, were preserved by his faithful friends, and thus remain to us at this day. Walafrid is but one out of many, whose

names are known in history, dedicated from the
earliest years to the cloister. St Boniface, Apostle
of Germany, was a monk at the age of five; St
Bede came to Wiremouth at the age of seven;
St Paul of Verdun is said by an old writer to have
left his cradle for the cloister; St Robert entered it
as soon as he was weaned; Pope Paschal the
Second was taken to Cluni, Ernof to Bec, the
Abbot Suger to St Denis, from their " most tender
infancy.

Infants can but gaze about at what surrounds
them, and their learning comes through their eyes.
In the instances we have been considering, their
minds would receive the passive impressions which
were made on them by the scene, and would be
moulded by the composed countenances and
solemn services which surrounded them. Such
was the education of these little ones, till perhaps
the age of seven; when, under the title of " pueri,"
they commenced their formal school-time, and
committed to memory their first lesson. That
lesson was the Psalter—that wonderful manual
of prayer and praise, which, from the time when
its various portions were first composed down to
the last few centuries, has been the most precious
viaticum of the Christian mind in its journey
through the wilderness. In early times St Basil
speaks of it as the popular devotion in Egypt,
Africa, and Syria; and St Jerome had urged its use
upon the Roman ladies whom he directed. All
monks were enjoined to know it by heart; the

young ecclesiastics learned it by heart; no bishop could be ordained without knowing it by heart; and in the parish schools it was learned by heart. The Psalter, with the Lord's Prayer and Creed, constituted the *sine qua non* condition of discipleship. At home pious mothers, as the Lady Helvidia, whom we have already introduced to the reader, taught their children the Psalter. It was only, then, in observance of a universal law, that the Benedictine children were taught it;—they mastered it, and then they passed into the secular school-room,—they next were introduced to the study of grammar."

By Grammar, it is hardly necessary to say, was not meant, as now, the mere analysis or rules of language, as denoted by the words etymology, syntax, prosody; but rather it stood for scholarship, that is, such an acquaintance with the literature of a language as implied the power of original composition and the *viva voce* use of it. Thus Cassiodorus defines it to be "skill in speaking elegantly, gained from the best poets and orators;" St Isidore, "the science of speaking well;" and Raban, "the science of interpreting poets and historians, and the rule of speaking and writing well." In the monastic school, the language of course was Latin; and in Latin literature first came Virgil; next Lucan and Statius; Terence, Sallust, Cicero; Horace, Persius, Juvenal; and of Christian poets, Prudentius, Sedulius, Juvencus, Aratus. Thus we find that the monks of St Alban's, near

Mayence, had standing lectures in Cicero, Virgil, and other authors. In the school of Paderborne there were lectures in Horace, Virgil, Statius, and Sallust. Theodulf speaks of his juvenile studies in the Christian authors, Sedulius and Paulinus, Aratus, Fortunatus, Juvencus, and Prudentius, and in the classical Virgil and Ovid. Gerbert, afterwards Sylvester the Second, after lecturing his class in logic, brought it back again to Virgil, Statius, Terence, Juvenal, Persius, Horace, and Lucan. A work is extant of St Hildebert's, supposed to be a school exercise; it is scarcely more than a cento of Cicero, Seneca, Horace, Juvenal, Persius, Terence, and other writers. Horace he must have almost known by heart.

Considering the number of authors which have to be studied in order to possessing a thorough knowledge of the Latin tongue, and the length to which those in particular run which are set down in the above lists, we may reasonably infer, that with the science of Grammar the Benedictine teaching began and ended, excepting, of course, such religious instruction as is rather the condition of Christian life than the acquisition of knowledge. At fourteen, when the term of boyhood was complete, the school-time commonly ended too, the lay youths left for their secular career, and the monks commenced the studies appropriate to their sacred calling. The more promising youths, however, of the latter class were suffered or directed first to proceed to further secular studies; and, in order to accompany them, we must take some more detailed view of the curriculum, of which Grammar was the introductory study.

This curriculum, derived from the earlier ages of heathen philosophy, was transferred to the use of the Church on the authority of St Augustine, who in his *De Ordine* considers it to be the fitting and sufficient preparation for theological learning. It is hardly necessary to refer to the history of its formation; we are told how Pythagoras prescribed the study of arithmetic, music, and geometry; how Plato and Aristotle insisted on grammar and music, which, with gymnastics, were the substance of Greek education; how Seneca speaks, though not as approving, of grammar, music, geometry, and astronomy, as the matter of education in his own day; and how Philo, in addition to these, has named logic and rhetoric. Augustine, in his enumeration of them, begins with arithmetic and grammar, including under the latter history; then he speaks of logic and rhetoric; then of music, under which comes poetry, as equally addressing the ear; lastly, of geometry and astronomy, which address the eye. The Alexandrians, whom he followed, arranged them differently—viz., grammar, rhetoric, and logic or philosophy, which branched off into the four mathematical sciences of arithmetic, music, geometry, and astronomy. And this order was adopted in Christian education, the first three sciences being called the Trivium, the last four the Quadrivium.

Grammar was taught in all these schools; but for those who wished to proceed further than the studies of their boyhood, seats of higher education had been founded by Charlemagne in the principal cities of his Empire, under the name of public schools, which may be considered the shadow, and even the nucleus of the universities which arose in a subsequent age. Such were the schools of Paris, Tours, Rheims, and Lyons in France; Fulda in Germany; Bologna in Italy. Nor did they confine themselves to the Seven Sciences above mentioned, though it is scarcely to be supposed that, in any science whatever, except grammar, they professed to impart more than the elements. Thus we read of St Bruno of Segni (A.D. 1080), after being grounded in the " litteræ humaniores," as a boy, by the monks of St Perpetuus near Aste, seeking the rising school of Bologna for the " altiores scientiæ." St Abbo of Fleury (A.D. 990), after mastering, in the monastery of that place, grammar, arithmetic, logic, and music, went to Paris and Rheims for philosophy and astronomy, and afterwards taught himself rhetoric and geometry. Raban, (A.D. 822) left the school of Fulda for a while for Alcuin's lectures, and learned Greek of a native of Ephesus. Walafrid (A.D. 840) passed from Richenau to Fulda. St William (A.D. 980), dedicated by his parents to St Benedict at St Michael's near Vercellæ, proceeded to study at Pavia. Gerbert (A.D. 990), one of the few cultivators of physics, after Fleury and Orleans, went to Spain.

St Wolfgang (A.D. 994), after private instruction, went to Richenau. Lupus (A.D. 840), after Ferrières, was sent for a time to Fulda. Fulbert too of Chârtres (A.D. 1000), though not a monk, may be mentioned as sending his pupils in like manner to finish their studies at schools of more celebrity than his own.

History furnishes us with specimens of the subjects taught in this higher education. We read of Gerbert lecturing in Aristotle's Categories and the Isagogæ of Porphyry; St Theodore taught the Anglo-Saxon youths Greek and mathematics; Alcuin, all seven sciences at York; and at some German monasteries there were lectures in Greek, Hebrew, and Arabic. The monks of St Benignus at Dijon gave lectures in medicine; the abbey of St Gall had a school of painting and engraving; the blessed Tubilo of that abbey was mathematician, painter, and musician. We read of another monk of the same monastery, who was ever at his carpentry when he was not at the altar, and of another who worked in stone. Hence Vitruvius was in repute with them. Another accomplishment was that of copying manuscripts, which they did with a perfection unknown to the scholastic age which followed them.

These manual arts, far more than the severer sciences, were the true complement of the Benedictine ideal of education, which, after all, was little more than a fair or a sufficient acquaintance with Latin literature. Such is the testimony of the ablest men of the time. "To pass from Grammar to Rhetoric, and then in course to the other liberal sciences," says Lupus, speaking of France, is "fabula tantum." It has ever been the custom in Italy," says Glaber Radulphus, writing of the year 1000, " to neglect all arts but Grammar." Grammar, moreover, in the sense in which we have defined it, is no superficial study, nor insignificant instrument of mental cultivation, and the school-task of the boy became the life-long recreation of the man. Amid the serious duties of their sacred vocation, the monks did not forget the books which had arrested and refined their young imagination. Let us return to the familiar correspondence of some of these more famous Benedictines, and we shall see what were the pursuits of their leisure, and the indulgences of their relaxation. Alcuin, in his letters to his friends, quotes Virgil again and again; he also quotes Horace, Terence, Pliny, besides frequent allusions to the heathen philosophers. Lupus quotes Horace, Cicero, Suetonius, Virgil, and Martial. Gerbert quotes Virgil, Cicero, Horace, Terence, and Sallust. Petrus Cellensis quotes Horace, Seneca, and Terence. Hildebert quotes Virgil and Cicero, and refers to Diogenes, Epictetus, Crœsus, Themistocles, and other personages of Greek history. Hincmar of Rheims quotes Horace. Paschasius Radbert's favourite authors were Cicero and Terence. Abbo of Fleury was especially familiar with Terence, Sallust, Virgil, and Horace; Peter the Venerable, with Virgil and

Horace; Hepidamn of St Gall took Sallust as a model of style.

Nor is their anxiety less to enlarge the range of their classical reading. Lupus asks Abbot Hatto through a friend for leave to copy Suetonius's *Lives of the Cæsars*, which is in the monastery of St Boniface in two small codices. He sends to another friend to bring with him the Catilinarian and Jugurthan Wars of Sallust, the Verrines of Cicero, and any other volumes which his friends happens to know either that he has not, or possesses only in faulty copies, bidding him withal beware of the robbers on his journey. Of another friend he asks the loan of Cicero's *De Rhetorica*, his own copy of which is incomplete, and of Aulus Gellius. In another letter he asks the Pope for Cicero's *De Oratore*, the *Institutions* of Quintillian, and the commentary of Donatus upon Terence. In like manner Gerbert tells Abbot Gisilbert that he has the beginning of the *Ophthalmicus* of the philosopher Demosthenes, and the end of Cicero's *Pro rege Deiotaro* ; and he wants to know if he can assist him in completing them for him. He asks a friend at Rome to send him by Count Guido the copies of Suetonius and Aurelius which belong to his archbishop and himself; he requests Constantine, the lecturer (*scholasticus*) at Fleury, to bring him Cicero's Verrines and *De Republica*, and he thanks Remigius, a monk of Treves, for having begun to transcribe for him the *Achilleid* of Statius, though he had been unable to proceed with it for want of

I

a copy.   To other friends he spoke of Pliny, Cæsar, and Victorinus.   Alcuin's Library contained Pliny, Aristotle, Cicero, Virgil, Statius, and Lucan; and he transcribed Terence with his own hand.

Not only the memory of their own youth, but the necessity of transmitting to the next generation what they had learned in it themselves, kept them loyal to their classical acquirements.   They were, in this aspect of their history, not unlike the fellows in our modern English universities, who first learn and then teach.   It is impossible, indeed, to overlook their resemblance generally to the elegant scholar of a day which is now waning, especially at Oxford, such as Lowth or Elmsley, Copleston or Keble, Howley or Parr, who thought little of science or philosophy by the side of the authors of Greece and Rome.   Nor is it too much to say, that the Colleges in the English Universities may be considered in matter of fact to be the lineal descendants or heirs of the Benedictine schools of Charlemagne.   The modern of course has vastly the advantage in the comparison; for he is familiar with Greek, has an exacter criticism and purer taste, and a more refined cultivation of mind.   He writes, verse at least, far better than the Benedictine, who had commonly little idea of it; and he has the accumulated aids of centuries in the shape of dictionaries and commentaries.   We are not writing a panegyric on the classical learning of the dark age, but describing what it was; and, with this object before us, we observe, that, what-

ever the monks had not, a familiar knowledge and
a real love they had of the great Latin writers,
and we assert moreover, that that knowledge and
love were but in keeping with the genius and character of their institute. For they instinctively
recognised in the graceful simplicity of Virgil or of
Horace, in his dislike of the great world, of political
contests and of ostentatious splendour, in his
unambitious temper and his love of the country,
an analogous gift to that religious repose, that
distaste for controversy, and that innocent cheerfulness which were the special legacy of St Benedict
to his children. This attachment to the classics
is well expressed by a monk of Paderborn, who,
when he would describe the studies of the place,
suffers his prose almost to dissolve into verse, as
he names his beloved authors,

Viguit Horatius,   magnus et Virgilius,
Crispus et Sallustius,   et urbanus Statius.

Ludusque fuit omnibus,   *insudare versibus,*
Et dictaminibus   *jucundisque cantibus.*

The latter of these stanzas, as they may be
called, illustrates what we have wished to express,
in speaking of the classical temperament of the
Benedictines. As far as they allowed themselves
in any recreation, which was not of a sacred nature,
they found it in these beautiful authors, who might
be considered as the prophets of the human race
in its natural condition. How strongly they contrast in this respect to the scholastic age which

swallowed them up! Amid the religious or ecclesiastical matters which were the subject of their
correspondence, questions of grammar and criticism are mooted, and a loving curiosity about the
nicety of languages is temperately indulged.
Whether *rubus* is masculine or feminine, is argued
from analogy and by induction; Ambrose makes it
feminine, and the names of trees, which have no
plurals, are feminine, as *populus, fraxinus ;* on the
other hand Virgil makes it masculine, and Priscian
allows it to be an exception to the rule.   Again, is
it *dispexeris* or *despexeris ?*   Priscian says *despicio*,
and makes *de* answer to the Greek κατὰ, *down ;* but
the Greek in the Psalm is, not κατίδῃς, but ὑπερίδῃς,
above.   Again, is the penultima of *voluerimus* long
or short? long, says Servius on Virgil.   They carry
their fidelity to the classics into their own poetical
compositions; far from resigning themselves to
that merely rhythmical versification, which is ever
grateful to the popular ear, which had been in use
from the Augustan era, and which afterwards
developed in *rhyme*, they rather affect the archaisms
and the licences of the classical era.   " Contraria
rerum," " genus omne animantum," " retundier,"
" formarier," " benedicier," " scribier," " in-
dupediret," "indunt,"savour of Ennius or Lucretius
rather than of Virgil.   They keep to the Augustans
metres, and they are never unwilling to use them.
Their theological treatises begin, their epistles to
kings end, with hexameters and pentameters.
They moralise, they protest, they soothe their

sorrows, they ask favours, they compile chronicles, they record their journeys, in heroics, elegiacs, and epigrams. They are versifiers, one and all, or at least those whose names or works are best known in history or in our libraries. The habit was formed at school, and it endured through life. Some indeed, as Lupus or Gerbert, had too many external occupations for the task; but others, as Theodulf, Bishop of Orleans, return to it in the evening of life, after the manner of Gregory Nazianzen in patristic times, or Lord Wellesley in our own. Bede, Alcuin, Aldhelm, Raban, Theodulf, Hildebert, Notgar, Adelhard, Walafrid, Agobard, Florus, Modoin, Heiric, Gerbert, Angilbert, Herman, Abbo, Odo, Huobald, Lupus, Fridouard, Paschasius, with many others, all wrote verse. We are not insinuating that they wrote it so happily as the Patriarch of Constantinople or the Governor-General of India; on the contrary, it was not their *forte ;* but Florus, for instance, is eloquent, and Walafrid Virgilian. Their subjects, when most sacred, are such as the great phenomena of nature, the country, woods, mountains, flocks and herds, plants, flowers, and others which we have called Benedictine. We cannot occupy our pages with extracts; but we are induced, as a specimen of what we mean by the alliance of St Benedict and Virgil, to quote the concluding lines of the Hortulus of Walafrid, which presents us a very pretty picture of an old monk amid children and fruit trees:—

" Hæc tibi servitii munuscula vilia parvi
Strabo tuus, Grimalde pater! . . .
Ut, cum conseptu viridis consederis horti,
Inter apricatas frondenti germine malos,
Persicus imparibus crines ubi dividit umbris,
Dum tibi cana legunt tenera lanugine poma
Ludentes pueri, schola lætabunda tuorum,
Atque volis ingentia mala capacibus indunt,
Grandia conantes includere corpora palmis,
Quo moneare habeas nostri, pater alme, laboris,
Dum relegis quæ dedo volens, interque legendum
Et vitiosa secas bonus, et placentia firmas."

We have taken a liberty with the last line, which
anyhow is somewhat feeble.

Their prose is superior to their verse; it has little
claim indeed to the purity of taste and of vocabu-
lary which we call classical; but it is good Latin
both in structure and in idiom. At anyrate the
change is wonderful, when we pass from the
Benedictine centuries to those which followed.

We take, for instance, a letter from Lupus to
Ebroin, Bishop of Poitiers, not because it is the
most favourable specimen of his style, but because
it is one of the shortest of his letters:—

" Causas meas Ludovico nostro significavi, quas
his litteris repetere superfluum duxi, cum eos, quæ
illi redditæ sunt, vos lecturos et velim et sciam.
Tantum postulo, ut in omnibus ita mihi adesse
dignemini, sicut me confidere illis etiam litteris
cognoscatis. Misi vobis eburneum pectinem, quem
quæso, ut in vestro retineatis usu, quo inter
pectendum arctior vobis mei memoria imprimatur."
—*Ep.* 39.

Or again, one of Gerbert's shortest, addressed to
some lawless freebooter, who had plundered the
abbey:—

" Recedant multa verba, et sequamur facta.
Sanctuarium Domini mei nec pecunia nec amicitia
vobis damus; nec, si datum est ab aliquo, con-
sentimus. Fœnum, quod vestri tulerunt, beato
Columbano restituite, si experiri non vultis, quid
possimus cum gratia domini nostri Cæsaris,
amicorum consilio et auxilio. His conditionibus
leges amicitiæ non refutamus."—*Ep.* 4.

We could not bring into a small compass any
comparison of the writers of the scholastic period
with those whom we are reviewing; a few sentences
out of each may not be considered to decide the
matter, yet at least they will illustrate, as far as
they go, what we have been saying. On the part
of the Benedictines, we have made our selection
almost at random: on the part of the Schoolmen,
we have attempted to find the most favourable
specimens.

For instance, Raban begins a chapter in the
third book of his *De Institutione Clericorum* with
the following sentence, which, whatever be thought
of it otherwise, is in structure and phrase fairly
Ciceronian:—

" De septem liberalibus artibus philosophorum,
ad quam utilitatem discendæ sunt catholicis, satis,
ut reor, superius diximus; illud adhuc adjicimus,
quod philosophi ipsi qui vocantur, si qua forte vera

et fidei nostræ accommodata in disputationibus suis seu scriptis dixerunt, maxime Platonici, non solum formidanda non sunt, sed ab eis etiam, tanquam injustis possessoribus, in usum nostrum vindicanda" (t. vi. p. 44).

Contrast with this a sentence from one of the *Opuscula* of St Thomas:—

" Nihil est homini amiabilius, libertate propriæ voluntatis.   Per hanc enim homo est etiam aliorum dominus; per hanc aliis uti vel frui potest; per hanc etiam actibus suis dominatur.   Unde, sicut homo dimittens divitias, vel personas conjunctas, eas abnegat, ita deserens propriæ voluntatis arbitrium, per quod ipse sui ipsius dominus est, se ipsum abnegare invenitur."—*Opusc.* 17, p. 400.

For a second contrast, let us on the one hand take Paschasius, who thus writes in the beginning of his commentary on St Matthew:—

" Unde nimirum Demetrius, Antiocho regi vim divinæ legis cum exponeret, aiebat, teste Josepho, quemdam Theopompum extitisse nomine, qui volens ex divinis litteris in sua historia quippiam contrectare, ilico mente turbatus fuit plus ferme triginta diebus, donec veniam vix precibus impetraret.   Ac deinde, quod ferit ei per visum cœlitus declaratum, hoc illi ideo accidisse, quoniam irreligiose divina scrutatus esset, atque hominibus ea proferre impuris vellet," etc.—*Bibl. Max. P.*, t. xiv. p. 358.

On the other hand Moneta, a contemporary of St Dominic:—

"Quod autem sit provisor animalium, patet secundum philosophos et in veritate. Dedit enim animalibus membra instrumentalia, et præter hoc intimavit eis modum utendi illis; alioquin, esset supervacaneum. . . . In quo apparet Dei providentiaetiam cum non utentibus ratione" (p. 502).

Now, we must not be imagined, in making this contrast, to have any disrespectful meaning as regards those great authors whose Latinity happens not to be equal to their sanctity or their intellectual power. Their merit, in respect to language, is of a different kind; it consists in their success in making the majestic and beautiful Latin tongue minister to scientific uses, for which it was never intended. But, because they have this merit of their own, that is no reason why we should deny to the writers who preceded them the praise of being familiar with the ancient language itself, a praise which is justly theirs, though seldom allowed to them. The writers of the Benedictine centuries are supposed to have the barbarism, without the science, of the Dominican period; and modern critics, who wish to be fair, seem to consider it a great concession, if they grant that an age must at least have some smattering in classical literature, which, as the foregoing pages show, is ever quoting it and referring to it. Thus Mr Hallam, in the opening chapter of his *Literature of Europe*, can but say, "Alcuin's own poems *could at least not* have been written by one *unacquainted* with Virgil." Again: "From this time, though *quotations* from

the Latin poets, especially Ovid and Virgil, and
sometimes from Cicero, are *not very* frequent, they
occur sufficiently to show that manuscripts had
been brought to *this* side of the Alps " (p. 7).
Some pages lower he says, quoting some of St
Adalhard's verses, " The quotation from Virgil in
the ninth century *perhaps deserves remark, though*
in one of Charlemagne's monasteries it is not by
any means *astonishing ;* " as if Virgil were not the
text-book in the northern schools, as our foregoing
quotations make clear, and ignorance, in that day,
when it was to be found, had not its special seat
in the southern side of the Alps, not in France and
Germany.   Passages such as these in men of wide
research simply perplex us. We ask ourselves
whether we have rightly understood their words,
or whether we read wrongly the historical facts
which they profess to be generalising. Perhaps it
is that we assume without warrant that the
quotations of Alcuin and the rest are *bona fide* such,
and not derived, as some have said, from catenas
of passages, commonplace books, or traditionary
use; * but such an account of them is absolutely

* " " Bede . . . had some familiarity with Virgil, Ovid,
Lucan, Statius, and even Lucretius. . . .   It may be
questioned, however, whether many of the citations from
ancient authors, often adduced from mediæval writers, as
indicating their knowledge of such authors, are more than
traditionary, almost proverbial, insulated passages, brilliant
fragments, broken off from antiquity, and reset again and
again by writers borrowing them from each other, but who
had never read another word of the lost poet, orator, or
philosopher."—Milman, *Latin Christ.*, vol. ii. p. 39.

inconsistent, first, with the testimonies which we have above cited, as to the actual studies of the young, and next, with the literary habits which those studies actually formed in the persons who were exercised in them. Can it be that critics of the nineteenth century, possessing the fine appreciation of classical poetry imparted in the public schools of England, glance their eye over the rude versification of Theodulf or Alcuin, and consider it the measure of the secular learning which gave it birth? M. Guizot, Protestant as he is, is a fairer and kinder judge of the cloister literature than Mr Hallam or Dean Milman.

And now to prevent misapprehension of our meaning in this review of the Benedictine schools, we have two remarks to make before we conclude, one on each side of the description to which that review has led us.

On the one hand, the classical studies and tastes which we have been illustrating, even though foreign to the monastic masses, as they may be called, even though historically traceable to the mission of St Theodore from the Holy See to England, must still be regarded a true offspring of the Benedictine discipline, and in no sense the result of seasons or places of relaxation and degeneracy. At first sight, indeed, there is some plausibility in saying that with the change of times a real change came over a portion of a great family of monks, and that, however usefully employed, Cassiodorus or Theodore, Alcuin or Walafrid, did certainly fall from their proper vocation, and did really leave it to Romuald, and others like him, to be, not only the most faithful imitators, but to be only true children of the ancient monachism. And, in confirmation of this view, it might be added, that the same circumstances which led the monks to literary pursuits, led them to political entanglements also, and that in the same persons, as Theodulf, Lupus, and Gerbert, learning and secular engagements were combined; and that, as no one would say that the cares of office were proper to a monk's vocation, as little could be fairly included in its classical attainments. Whatever be the best mode of treating this difficulty, which of course demands a candid and equitable consideration, here, in addition to what we have said by the way, we shall make one answer of different kind, which seems to us conclusive, and there leave the question. When, then, we are asked whether these studies are but the accidents and the signs of a time of religious declension, we reply that they are found in those very persons, on the contrary, who were pre-eminent in devotional and ascetic habits, and who were so intimately partakers in the spirit of mortification, whether of St Benedict or St Romuald, that they have come down to us with the reputation of saints,—nay, have actually received canonisation or beatification. Theodore himself is a saint; Alcuin and Raban are styled "beati"; Hildebert is "venerable"; Bede and Aldhelm are saints; and we can say the same of

St Angilbert, St Abbo, St Bertharius, St Adalhard, St Odo, and St Paschasius Radbert. At least Catholics must feel the full force of this argument; for they cannot permit themselves to attribute any dereliction of vocation to those whom the Church holds up as choice specimens of divine power, and, as being such, miraculously sealed for eternal bliss.

This is our remark on one side the question; on the other, it must not of course be supposed—indeed our last remark negatives the idea—that critical scholarship or classical erudition was the business of life, even in the case of this minority of the monastic family, who took so prominent a part in the education of their time. We have distinctly said, that, after their school years, the monks were as little taken up with the classics, *exceptis excipiendis*, as members of parliament or country gentlemen at the present day. They had their serious engagements, as statesmen have now, though of a different kind, and to these they gave themselves. Theology was their one study; to theology secular literature ministered, first as an aid and an ornament, then as a relaxation, amid the mental exertion which it involved. Nor was this literature cultivated without some holy jealousy on the part of the cultivators; "nuces pueris";—there was a time of life when it ought to be put aside; there was even a danger of its seductiveness. Alcuin himself, if we may trust the account, reproved on one occasion the study, at least of the poets; and in one of his extant letters he complains of a former pupil, then raised to the episcopate, for preferring Virgil to his old master Flaccus, that is, himself, and prays that " the four Gospels, not the twelve Æneids, may fill his breast " (*Ep.* 129). St Paschasius too, in spite of his love for Terence and Cicero, expresses a judgment, in one passage of his comment upon Ezekiel (*Bibl. Max. P.*, t. xiv. p. 788), against the elder monks being occupied with the heathen poets and philosophers. Lanfranc, when an Irish Bishop asked him some literary question, made answer, " Episcopale propositum non decet operam dare hujusmodi studiis; we passed in these our time of youth, but, when we took on ourselves the pastoral care, we bade them farewell " (*Ep.* 33). The instance of Pope Gregory is well known; when the Bishop of Vienne had been led to lecture in the classics, he wrote, " A fact has come to our ears, which we cannot name without a blush, that you, my brother, lecture on literature " (grammatica).— *Ep.* xi. 54. Such occupations, indeed, were in those centuries generally and reasonably held to be inconsistent with the calling of a Bishop. St Jerome speaks as strongly in an earlier age.

What was true of the Bishop was on the whole true of the monk also; he might perhaps have special duties as the *scholasticus* of his monastery, but ordinarily, while his manual labour was either in the field or in the *scriptorium*, so his intellectual exercises were for the most part combined with his devotional, and consisted in the study of the sacred volume. This was mainly what at that time was meant by theology. " Theologia, hoc est, Scripturarum meditatio," says Thomassin (*Disc. Eccl.*, t. ii. p. 288). Their theology was a loving study and exposition of Holy Scripture, according to the teaching of the Fathers, who had studied and expounded it before them. It was a loyal adherence to the teaching of the past, a faithful inculcation of it, an anxious transmission of it to the next generation. In this respect it differed from the theology of the times before and after them. Patristic and scholastic theology each involved a creative action of the intellect; that this is the case as regards the Schoolmen, need not be proved here; nor is it less true, though in a different way, of the Theology of the Fathers. Origen, Tertullian, Athanasius, Chrysostom, Augustine, Jerome, Leo, are authors of powerful, original minds, and engaged in the production of original works. There is no greater mistake, surely, than to suppose that a revealed truth precludes originality in the treatment of it. The contrary is acknowledged in the case of secular subjects, in which it is the very triumph of originality not to invent or discover what perhaps is already known, but to make old things read as if they were new, from the novelty of aspect in which they are placed. This faculty of investing with associations, of applying to particular purposes, of deducing consequences, of impressing upon the imagination, is creative; and though false associations, applications, deductions, and impressions are often made, and were made by some theologians of the early Church, such as Origen and Tertullian, this does not prove that originality is not co-extensive with truth. And so in like manner as to Scripture; to enter into the mind of the sacred author, to follow his train of thought, to bring together to one focus the lights which various parts of Scripture throw upon his text, and to give adequate expression to the thoughts thus evolved, in other words, the breadth of view, the depth, or the richness, which we recognise in certain early expositions, is a creation. Nor is it an inferior faculty to discriminate, rescue, and adjust the truth, which a fierce controversy threatens to tear in pieces, at a time when the ecclesiastical atmosphere is thick with the dust of the conflict, when all parties are more or less in the wrong, and the public mind has become so bewildered as not to be able to say what it does or what it does not hold, or even what it held before the strife of ideas began. In such circumstances, to speak the word evoking order and peace, and to restore the multitude of men to themselves and to each other, by a reassertion of what is old with a luminousness of explanation which is new, is a gift inferior only to that of revelation itself.

This gift is not the characteristic of the history, nor is it akin to the spirit or the object, as we have described them, of the Benedictine Order. At the time of which we are writing, the Christian athlete, after running one length of the stadium, was taking breath before commencing a second course: the Christian combatant was securing his conquests in the wide field of thought by a careful review and catalogue of them, before going forth to make new ones. He was fitly represented, therefore, at such a season by the Benedictine, faithful, conscientious, affectionate, and obedient, like the good steward who keeps an eye on all his master's goods, and preserves them from waste or decay. First, then, he compared, emendated, and transcribed the text of Scripture; next he transcribed the Fathers who directly or indirectly commented on it; then he attached to its successive portions such passages from the Fathers as illustrated them; then he fused those catenated passages into one homogeneous comment of his own: and there he stopped. He seldom added anything original. In such a task the skill would lie in the happy management and condensation of materials brought together from very various quarters, and here he would find the advantage of the literary habits gained in his early education. A taste for criticism would be another result of it, which we see in Bede, and which would result in so much of leaning to the literal interpretation of Scripture as was consistent with the profession of editing and republishing, as it may be called, the comments of the Fathers. We see this tendency in Alcuin, Paschasius, and especially in Druthmar. Indeed, Alcuin's greatest work was the revision of the Scripture

K

text. Other commentators were Ansbert, Sma-
ragdus, Haymo, Remi, and the Irish Sedulius, if
he was a Benedictine. The most widely celebrated, however, of these works was the *Glossa
Ordinaria* of Walafrid, which was in great measure
an abridgment of Rabina's Catena, and became a
standard authority in the centuries which followed.

But times were approaching when such peaceful
labours were not sufficient for the Church's need,
and when theology needed to be something more
than the rehearsal of what her champions had
achieved and her sages had established in ages
passed away. As the new Christian society, which
Charlemagne inaugurated, grew, its intellect grew
with it, and at last began to ask questions and
propose difficulties, which *catenæ* and commentaries
could not solve. Hard-headed objectors were not
to be subdued by the reverence for antiquity and
the amenities of polite literature; and, when
controversies arose, the Benedictines found themselves, from the necessity of the times, called to
duties which were as uncongenial to the spirit of
their founder as the political engagements of St
Dunstan or St Bernard. Nor must it be supposed
that the other parts of Christendom did not furnish
matters demanding their theological acumen, even
though none had arisen in the Frankish churches
themselves. And here, we conceive, we have this
remarkable confirmation of the identity of the
Benedictine character, that, in proportion as these
matters were in substance already decided by the

Fathers, they acquitted themselves well in the controversy, and in proportion as these matters demanded some original explanations, the monastic disputants were less successful. And in speaking of them, we speak of course of their age itself, of which they were leading teachers, and which they represent. And we speak, not of individual monks, who would have the natural talents, the intellectual acuteness and subtlety of other men, but of the action of the monasteries, considered as bodies and historically, which is the true measure of the mental discipline to which their Rule subjected them. We speak of those whose duty lay, by virtue of their vocation, not in confronting doubts but in suppressing them, and who were not likely on the whole to succeed in exercises of reason in which they had no practice.

One of the countries to which we allude, as being at the era of Charlemagne the seat of theological error, was Spain, then under the power of the Saracens. The victorious infidels, in spite of their general toleration of Catholicism, of course could not avoid inflicting on it the most serious injuries. One of these was the decay or destruction of its schools, and the want of education in its priesthood, which was the consequence. Another injury lay in the circumstance that Mahometanism, being a misbelief or heresy, more than a direct denial of the faith, seemed to have a right to interfere with it, and had a tendency to corrupt it by the insinuation of its own opinions and traditions about

Christian facts and doctrines. Mahomet is said to have been indebted to the teaching of a Nestorian monk, and the demolition of images was one of the watchwords of his armies. Now, from Spain at this time proceeded the heresy of the Adoptionists, which is of a Nestorian character; and it was in Spain that Claudius of Turin matured those uncatholic opinions, especially on the subject of images, which have given him a place in ecclesiastical history.

The conflict with Nestorianism had been completed long before the time of Charlemagne; accordingly the theologians of the age, in refuting it, had but to repeat the arguments which they found ready for them in the pages of the Fathers. Alcuin was one of those who undertook the controversy, and proved himself abundantly prepared for the work. "Paulinus and Alcuin," says Professor Dölinger, "proved their point with a degree of theological acumen, and with a knowledge of the Fathers, which in that age may surprise us."

Such was their success, when the doctrine in question had already been defined; but, on the other hand, the question with which Claudius's name is connected, the honour due to images, was still *sub judice*, and when the ecumenical decision came from Nicæa, from whatever cause, the Franks misunderstood and disputed it. The same great council of Frankfort, which condemned the Adoptionists, acted as a protection to the Iconoclasts of Constantinople. We are far indeed from insinuating that the Fathers of the Frankish churches really differed from the definition which came to them from the East; but even for a century afterwards those churches regarded it, to say the least, with dissatisfaction.

Meanwhile the spirit of inquiry was alive and operative even within the hearts of these peaceful monastic communities themselves. We find it, as it would seem, in one of the immediate friends and pupils of Alcuin. Fridegis, of the school of York, to whom he addressed various of his letters and works, and whom he made his successor at Tours, has left behind him an argumentative fragment of so strange a nature that it has been thought a mere exercise in disputation and not a portion of a serious work. He starts, moreover, with a proposition in favour of the supremacy of reason as contrasted with authority, which, though admitting of a Catholic explanation, is capable also of being made the basis of a philosophy to which we shall immediately have occasion to allude. Soon after, Gotteschalc, a monk of Orbais, taught that the decree of divine predestination has direct reference to the lost as well as the saved; and about the same time Ratramn of the monastery of Corbie opposed the Catholic doctrine of the Holy Eucharist. But these intellectual movements within the Benedictine territory were eclipsed by a manifestation of the sceptical spirit which came from a country, where from its prevalent religious temperament such a phenomenon was little to have been expected.

There was a portion of the Western Church which
had never been included in the Roman Empire,
and but partially, if at all, included within the range
of the Benedictine discipline. While that discipline
made its way northward, became the instrument
of Anglo-Saxon conversion, and even supplanted
the rule of Columban in the French monasteries,
the countrymen of Columban remained faithful
to their old monachism, descended southwards a
second time, and retaliated on the convents of the
Continent by a fresh introduction of themselves
and their traditions. At this period, whatever
may have been their literary attainments, they
were more remarkable for a bold independence of
mind, a curiosity, activity, and vigour of thought,
which contrasted strongly with the genius of Bede
and Raban. Their strength lay in those exercises
of pure reason which go by the name of "philosophy," or of "wisdom." Thus in an ancient
writer the Irish Scots are spoken of as "*sophia
clari.*" By Heric of Auxerre, in the passage so
often quoted, they are described as "*philosophorum
greges,*" venturing across the stormy sea to the
wide continent of Europe. And so in the legendary
account, by a monk of St Gall, of the Irish scholars
who accosted the Frankish Emperor, they are
represented as crying out, "Who wants *wisdom?*
who will buy *wisdom?*" Dunstan, again, is said
to have learned "*philosophy*" in Ireland; and
Benedict of Aniane, the second founder of the
Benedictines, is expressly described as looking with

suspicion on their syllogistic method, which was so
hostile to the habits of mind which his own Order
cultivated. These Irish scholars, indeed, were too
sincere Catholics, viewing them in the mass, to
warrant this jealousy; but it was not without
foundation, as we shall see, as regards individuals,
and at least would have abundant warrant in the
judgments of those who differed so much from
them in mental characteristics as did the Benedictines. On the other hand, there was much in
the Anglo-Saxon temper intimately congenial with
the latter: then, as now, the occupants of the
British soil seem to have been practical rather
than speculative, fond of hard work rather than of
hard thought, tenacious of what they had received,
jealous of novelty, the champions of law and order.
Thus the English and Irish may be said so far to
represent respectively the two great Orders which
came in succession on the stage of ecclesiastical
history; and, as they were not without their
collisions at home, so we detect some instances,
and may conjecture others, of their rivalry as missionaries and teachers in central Europe. We read,
for instance, in the history of St Boniface, that one
of his antagonists in his organisation of the
Churches which he had founded in Germany, was
an Irish priest of the name of Clement. Boniface
relates, if his account is to be received to the letter,
that this priest neither allowed the authority of
Jerome, Augustin, or Gregory, nor of the sacred
canons; that he maintained the marriage of

bishops; argued from Scripture in defence of
marriage with a sister-in-law, and taught a sort
of universalism. Another Irishman, with whom
Boniface had a quarrel, was Virgil, afterwards
Bishop of Salzburg, who had been acknowledged,
as well as Boniface, for a saint. He offended
Boniface by maintaining what seems like a
doctrine of the existence of *antipodes*.

The antagonism between the two schools extended into the next century. Of course John
Scotus Erigena, whom Charles the Bald placed in
the chair of Alcuin in the School of the Palace, is
the palmary specimen of the philosphical party
among the Irish monks. This remarkable man,
while acknowledging the authority of Revelation,
laid it down as a first principle of his speculations,
as Fridegis had done before him, that reason must
come first, and authority second. Such a proposition indeed was faulty only in its application; for
St Austin himself had laid it down in his treatise
De Ordine. It is self-evident that we should not
know what was Revelation and what was not,
unless we used our reason to decide the point.
Whatever we are obliged in the event to learn
from external sources, our process of inquiry must
begin from within. The ancient Father whom
we have mentioned propounds both the principle
and the sense in which it is true. " We learn
things necessarily in two ways," he says, " by
authority and by reason. Tempore auctoritas, re
autem ratio prior est; " but Erigena, as is generally

agreed, accounted reason, not only as the ultimate basis of religious truth, but the direct and proper warrant for it; and, armed with this principle, he proceeded to take part in the two controversies which we have already had occasion to mention, the Predestinarian and the Eucharistic. "The writings have come to us," says the church of Lyons, speaking of his tendencies, like Clement's, to universalism, "the writings have come to us, *vaniloqui et garruli hominis*, who, disputing on divine prescience and predestination with human, or, as he boasts, philosophical reasonings, without any deference to Scripture, or regard to the authority of the Holy Fathers, has dared to define by his own independent assertion what is to be held and followed." Thus Erigena adopted Clement's argumentative basis, as well as his doctrine. His views upon reason and authority are distinctly avowed in the first book of his work *De divisione naturæ*. "You are not ignorant," he argues "that what is *prius natura* ranks higher than what is *prius tempore*. We have been taught," referring apparently to St Austin, "that reason is prior in nature, authority in time; now, whereas nature was created together with time, authority did not begin with the beginning of time and nature; on the other hand, reason had its origin with nature and time in the first beginning of things." The Scholar replies to him, "Reason itself teaches this; for authority has proceeded from right reason, reason by no means from authority. For all authority which is not approved by right reason is weak; whereas right reason, when it is fortified in its own strength, settled and immovable, need not be corroborated by the concurrence of any authority " (lib. i. n. 71). In like manner, in the commencement of his work on Predestination, while appealing to St Austin, he makes philosophy and religion convertible terms.

Erigena was succeeded in the Schola Palatii by Mannon, who inherited his master's philosophy. He himself had called Plato the greatest of philosophers, and Aristotle the most subtle of investigators; and, according to the testimony of Friar Bacon, he was a successful interpreter of the latter writer; and Mannon, in like manner, has left commentaries on Plato's *De Legibus* and *De Republica* and on Aristotle s *Ethics*. About the same time flourished in France another Irishman, named Macarius; and he too showed the same leaning towards pantheism which has been imputed to Erigena. From him this error was introduced into the monastery of Corbie. At a later date we hear of one Patrick, who from his name may be considered as an Irishman, holding the same heterodox opinion about the Eucharist which Ratramn and Erigena advanced.

As to the two controversies, which have been mentioned more than once, while they exemplify to us the *scholasticismus ante scholasticos* then in action, they afford fresh illustrations also of the insufficiency of such instruments as the Church at that time had in her service, to meet this formidable antagonist of her religious supremacy. No mind equal to Erigena appeared on the side of traditionary teaching; and the vigour with which the Adoptionists were condemned and the *Filioque* inserted in the Creed, did not manifest itself in the dealing of the Frankish Synods with the bold doctrine of Gotteschalc and Ratramn. Gotteschalc, as we have said, was a monk of Orbais. We suddenly find him asserting categorically that the reprobate have been predestined to damnation from eternity. Raban and the Synod of Mentz condemned this doctrine. Hincmar and the Synod of Quiercy condemn it also; and Pardulus, Bishop of Laon, writes against it. Then Lupus writes, if not in defence of Gotteschalc, at least not in accordance with Hincmar, who, in distress for a champion, has recourse to no other than Erigena, and Erigena, as might be expected from what has been said above, proceeded to commit himself to an extreme doctrine of universalism, as Gotteschalc had to an extreme predestinarianism. Upon this, Florus and Prudentius write against Erigena; and Remigius, explaining or espousing the thesis of Gotteschalc, writes against the three Epistles of Raban, Hincmar, and Pardulus. Hincmar replies in a second Synod of Quiercy; and the Bishops of Lorraine rejoin in the Synod of Valence. The controversy ceases rather than terminates at the Synod of Savonnières, in which all parties were represented, and in which four important articles

were received, bearing indirectly on the subject of
dispute, but leaving without distinct notice the
original position of Gotteschalc.

In the eucharistic controversy, which lasted
through several centuries, the Benedictine Paschasius, supported by Haimo, Hincmar, and
Ratherius, expounded the traditionary doctrine
afterwards defined; but his statements were met
by the dissent, or the hesitation, as it would appear,
of men of his own schools, Raban, Ratramn,
Amalarius, Heribald, Heriger, Druthmar, and
Florus. At the end of two centuries indeed
appeared the great Benedictines, Lanfranc and
Anselm, who dealt successfully with this as well as
other controversies. But it must be recollected
that, although their school of Bec is confessedly
the historical fountainhead of the new theology
which was making its way into Christendom, it is
as little a fair specimen of the Benedictine character in matters of teaching, as such imperial
minds as their brother-monk and contemporary
Hildebrand, can fairly represent their institute in
ecclesiastical politics.

And thus the period, properly Benedictine,
ended; this honour being shown by Providence to
the great Order from which it is named, in reward
for its long and patient services to religion, that,
though its monks were not to be immediately
employed by the Church in the special sense in
which they had been her ministers for some
hundreds of years, still they should be the first

to point out, and they should hansel, those new weapons, which an Order of a different genius was destined to wield against a new description of opponents.

Nor is it without significancy that the Anglo-Saxon Church, itself the creation of the Benedictines, and the seat from which their influence went out for the education or conversion of Europe from the Baltic to the Bay of Biscay, should have its share in this honour; and that, as Theodore was brought all the way from Tarsus to Canterbury, so Lanfranc from Lombardy, and Anselm from Piedmont, should successively fill the archi-episcopal throne of Theodore.

THE END

EDINBURGH
COLSTON AND CO. LTD.
PRINTERS